FORGET THE MEMORIES

by
Clifford E. Isaacson

Compiled by
Kevin Isaacson

In loving memory of Clifford E. Isaacson

Contents

FORWARD

I KNEW SHORTLY after my dad, Clifford Isaacson, passed away on January 22, 2015, that I couldn't just let his years of work fade into the past. Maybe it was out of love. Maybe it was out of pride. Maybe it was because I, as well as my siblings, was the basis for his research so I felt a special connection to what he had discovered.

His discoveries in birth order weren't by design. This world has a way of leading us down roads at the exact right time and only at that time. Things happen for a reason. This happened for a reason.

Were we the perfect family? Absolutely not. Did our dad, along with our loving mother, raise us perfectly because he had all of this knowledge? Absolutely not. My dad did not always have this knowledge at his fingertips. He didn't have all of the answers. He observed closely and continued to learn more and more about us as we grew. His passion was learning these fascinating dynamics and passing along that knowledge. From what he observed in our family, he was able to relate and spot patterns in how those same dynamics appeared in others.

My dad touched many lives throughout his years of ministry and counseling. He learned as much from each person that he helped as they did from him. He not only learned, he recorded and compiled that knowledge so that others may learn from it as well.

Thinking inside the box was not a concept that my dad found appealing. He did not settle for traditional thinking as it related to counseling or birth order. He forged new pathways in both arenas and we are all that much better off because of his drive, passion, insight, and curiosity.

This book is a compilation of notes, social media posts, and articles that my dad wrote. I hope that you enjoy learning more about yourself and others as you move along on your journey through these pages.

~ Kevin Isaacson

EVERYDAY PSYCHOLOGY

EVERYONE USES SOME psychology in everyday life. People use it to understand themselves, to do better, to relate to others, to parent their children, to get along with others at work, and to make sense of family. I have had the good fortune of hearing from thousands of clients over the past forty years of the everyday psychology they use to live their lives. It is this everyday psychology that I want to share.

Everyday psychology is developed by people in the process of living. It's the wisdom that older people pass on to younger people, grandparents to grandchildren, mentors to mentees, and teachers to students. It is wisdom that comes from figuring things out rather than from clinical studies by professors who put their findings into complicated words. It is psychology that is in common sense, street smarts, and insight. We enrich each other's lives everyday with this psychology.

BE YOUR OWN THERAPIST

MEMORIES DRIVE EMOTIONAL, mental, physical, and behavioral problems. The power of these memories disappears when you tell yourself out loud, "Forget that memory." Here's how you can use that tool:

Emotionally – when you are feeling a bad feeling, say to yourself out loud, "Forget that memory." Use it with anxiety, guilt, shyness, anger, hopelessness, worry, sadness, boredom, etc.

Mental – when you get a bad thought, say to yourself out loud, "Forget that memory. Use it with thoughts of doing something wrong, hurting someone, doing something dishonest, getting even, cheating, destroying something, doing something ugly, betraying someone, lying, accusing someone, trying to scare someone, trying to control someone, etc.

Addictions – to turn off an unwelcome addictive urge, say aloud to yourself, "Forget that memory." Use it when you have an urge to smoke a cigarette, to gamble, to eat when you're not hungry, to drink alcohol, to shop, to engage in harmful behavior, etc.

Physical – use it for physical ailments that may be psychological in origin. Tell yourself aloud, "Forget that memory" when you feel pain, stiffness, aching, shaking, headaches, sinus problems, symptoms of illness, etc.

Compulsive behavior – use it to overcome bad habits by telling yourself out loud, "Forget that memory." Use it with cursing, nail biting, speeding, stealing, bad gestures, hurrying, procrastinating, failing to fix things, lying, putting others down, ignoring feelings, laziness, criticizing, etc.

Note: Anything we say out loud goes into the subconscious so we create our own world by what we say out loud. As soon as you say something you regret, follow it up by telling yourself out loud, "Forget that memory."

LEARNING NATURALLY

LEARNING IS NATURAL. Most things we learn, we learn naturally from experience. But there are blocks in our childhood memories that make learning a struggle, especially when you need to learn something, like in school. Just deciding to learn something triggers memories to make leaning difficult.

The most common memory that blocks learning is touching the hot stove. That hurt. Someone informed you at that moment that you have to learn not to touch the hot stove. This left you with a memory that says, "Learning is painful," like touching a hot stove.

Another common memory that hinders learning has to do with when you did something that turned out badly. Perhaps you hurt yourself, broke something, or had to start over. Someone connected that learning experience with pain, telling you, "That'll teach you!" Again, that memory contributed to your difficulty with learning.

On the other hand, if you don't know you are learning, these memories do not affect you. It's only when you start to learn something on purpose that the memories kick in that make you think that learning is painful. And of course, if learning is painful, it is to be avoided. Learning that cannot be avoided, like school, creates inner conflict between learning and trying to avoid pain. That's why so many students do not like school.

To set yourself free from the fear of painful learning, remember the memory of touching the hot stove, of hearing someone tell you to learn not to touch the hot stove, and then tell yourself to forget that memory. Also, tell yourself to forget those memories of being told, "That will teach you!" The memories will be neutralized by your subconscious so they no longer obstruct learning.

Learning is a fun adventure when the fear of pain is gone. You'll be surprised at how interesting life is when you are free to learn.

COMMUNICATION OF FACTS

COMMUNICATION OCCURS ON two levels, facts and meaning.

There are obstacles to communication that come from childhood memories. The obstacles to communicating facts are with listening and talking. Talking communicates facts, listening hears the facts.

The problems with talking come from memories of someone telling you not to interrupt. You may have had something important to say but you were told not to talk. This left you with a subconscious memory that keeps you from saying something because you may be interrupting someone else's talking. The stronger the subconscious memory, the more likely you are to not tell others facts that may be important.

Because this is so common, it is important to allow periods of silence when you are talking with someone so that person finds the right time to tell you something, the right time being when you are not talking.

To set yourself free to talk, tell yourself to "forget those memories that make you talk" because they will trigger the memories that won't let you talk. To reinforce your freedom to talk, tell yourself, "Remember those memories that let you talk." You can use these statements to help others as well.

Listening also has its obstacles in subconscious memory. The memory comes from being lectured by someone until you became tired of listening, and began to think of other things, such as what you would like to be doing instead. As these memories kick in now, your mind will wander off instead of paying attention to what someone is telling you.

To enable listening tell yourself to "forget those memories that make you listen" so they don't trigger the memories that do not let you listen. And, tell yourself to "remember those memories that let you listen" because you have such memories that need to be reinforced.

You'll be surprised by how much more you will learn by being able to talk and listen.

COMMUNICATION OF MEANING

COMMUNICATION OCCURS ON two levels, facts and meaning.

There are obstacles to communication that come from childhood memories. The obstacles to communicating meaning are with explaining and understanding. Explaining conveys meaning, understanding receives meaning.

The obstacles to explaining come from being forced to explain as a child. This kind of explaining is self-defense, as you try to get the other person to understand so they will not be angry at you. This kind of explaining rarely works because the adult will usually reject your explanation in favor of what they already believe.

Being forced to explain creates memories that will make the adult explain in self-defense or else keep the adult from explaining something for fear of rejection. To neutralize these memories tell yourself to "forget those memories that make you explain."

On the other hand, you have done constructive explaining when you enabled someone to understand something. This happens when you teach someone to do something, use something, or to learn something. To reinforce these memories, tell yourself to "remember those memories that let you explain."

There are also obstacles to understanding that result in jumping to conclusions. As a child, you may have been asked in an angry tone, "Do you understand?" You knew you were to understand without further explanation. You had to say you understood. When this memory kicks in, it makes you jump to a conclusion without hearing all of the explanation. This memory keeps you from really understanding. To neutralize it, tell yourself to "forget the memories that make you understand."

On the other hand, you have understood things by listening to the full explanation, perhaps even asking questions to clarify your understanding. To reinforce these memories, tell yourself to "remember those memories that let you understand."

Good explaining and understanding can enrich relationships greatly.

EXPAND YOUR PERSONALITY

DO YOU FEEL like other people have more freedom to do things than you do? There might be things that you would like to do but something in you interferes. Perhaps there are blocks to doing things, beliefs that you cannot do them, or somehow it just isn't you. You cannot say what you want, you cannot relate in ways that you want , or you cannot do what is good for you. Without knowing it, you may have blocked many resources in yourself.

The blocking comes about when you dislike someone else, even if you dislike them for good reason. When you dislike someone, your subconscious automatically rejects whatever parts in you resemble that person. If you dislike enough people, you have rejected large parts of yourself. You need to recover those parts.

You cannot decide to like people whom you dislike without inner conflict. What you can do is decide that it is okay for you to be like that person without having to do things the way they do. For instance, let's say that the other person hits other people with his hand. When you decide you do not want to be like that person, you give up the use of your hand so you don't hit people. But you need your hand for many things. You can decide it is okay for you to have your hand but to use it differently, using it in your own way.

When you tell yourself it is okay to be someone, the response is liberation on the subconscious level. You may not notice any changes immediately on the conscious level,

17

but if you pay attention you may find yourself with a new freedom to do things. The subconscious opens doors to the resources that you have had locked up.

Realize that each time you dislike someone that is an opportunity for you to tell yourself "It is okay to be like that person." The more you take advantage of those opportunities, the more resources you will have to draw on for what you want to do. You may surprise yourself.

LISTENING TO YOURSELF

SUBCONSCIOUSLY LISTENING TO yourself helps keep your mind straight. Most of us listen to ourselves and talk to ourselves. This inner conversation enables us to process incoming information as well as access what we already know.

You might have learned not to listen to yourself if you had several older siblings who did not listen to you but who also overrode what you said so that parents did not listen either. They might have called you stupid, implying that what you could say was not worth saying. You decided that it was best not to say anything that might be stupid and no one was going to listen anyway. It was no use having something to say if no one was going to listen. This became a subconscious memory to not listen to yourself.

Confusion is the result of not listening to yourself. Your subconscious does a great job of figuring things out that you need to hear. If you are not listening to yourself, you cannot access what your subconscious wants you to know. Participation in conversation becomes difficult because you have nothing to contribute. In desperation, you may make up things to say because nothing comes to mind from your subconscious.

To relate well to yourself and others, it needs to be okay for you to listen to yourself. To liberate yourself from these early memories of no one listening, you can tell your subconscious to forget those memories. In addition, you can tell your subconscious that it is okay for you to listen to yourself. Fortunately, your subconscious listens when you talk to it.

As you become free to listen to yourself, you'll find things coming to mind that you need to know. Your insight into situations, people, interactions, and your own motivations will grow.

Not being listened to may have left you with anger. You may discover a dramatic decrease in the anger as you listen to yourself. Your anger came from blaming others for not listening to you, especially if they showed any sign of not understanding what you were saying. Now you know that the problem was with memories in you, not in their behavior toward you.

As you listen to yourself you'll hear a lot. Enjoy your new communication skills.

HOW TO FEEL GOOD WHEN THINGS ARE BAD

HOW CAN YOU feel good when things are bad? Although you may realize that no matter how bad you feel, your feelings will not change anything. Still, you cannot stop from feeling bad. It may seem that before you can feel good, things will have to change. Not so. It is possible to feel good when things are bad.

Bad feelings can come from early memories rather than from our circumstances. You see, we live from our subconscious memories. Our memories drive our feelings, our thoughts, our actions, and our interactions. Our memories determine how we interpret things. Everything we do is memory driven. You are able to read what I write because you have memories that allow you to understand the language in which it is written. If it were written in Russian, you could not understand it because you do not have the memories to draw on. If you do have the memories to draw on, you can read Russian. Understanding the effect of subconscious memories reveals the secret of how to feel good when things are bad.

What are the memories that make us feel bad? Actually, these memories are from when you got things done by feeling bad. When you were an infant in the crib, you could not get something to eat when you got hungry, change your diaper when you became uncomfortable, or stop the pin from sticking you. You reacted by feeling bad, i.e., crying, and someone came to meet your need. In your developing mind, you stored the memory that told you that you can get things done by feeling bad. It is from that stored memory that bad feelings come from.

Here's how those memories from the crib make us feel bad now. We face a difficult situation that is beyond our control. There seems to be nothing we can do, to which the subconscious responds by saying in effect, "I know what to do. If we feel bad enough, long enough, that will take care of it." So feeling bad is a way of trying to fix things you can't fix any other way.

So how do we get out of feeling bad? We talk to ourselves. We tell ourselves it is okay to feel okay even though things are the way they are. The subconscious decides to give up feeling bad, in effect saying "We are not going to fix things by feeling bad so we need to find another way to get things done." Once that decision is made on the subconscious level, you begin to feel better, become aware of other possibilities in your situation, confirming that the subconscious is doing more than having you feel bad to get things done.

There is a question that brings this issue to focus. The question is, "Is it okay for you to feel okay, even though things are the way they are?" The subconscious mind waits for your answer of "yes" to that question to experience the freedom of more effective ways to get things done.

HOW TO FEEL GOOD

NATURALLY

THERE ARE NATURAL ways to feel good. Unfortunately, many of us were taught artificial ways to feel good by well-meaning adults when we were children.

It happened something like this. You were six years-old, having a bad day, dragging emotionally, a tear running down your cheek. Grandma was watching, felt bad for you, and decided to do something to help you feel better. Next thing you know, she is giving you a cookie and a glass of milk, telling you that the cookie and milk will make you feel better. You eat the cookie, drink the milk, and sure enough, you feel better. You just learned things from Grandma that would give you trouble in years to come as you live from this memory.

The first idea you got from Grandma was that you always have to feel good. She did not put her arm around you, let you know that you will have bad days, and comfort you. Instead, by giving you the milk and cookie, she made you believe that you had to feel good.

The second idea you got from Grandma was that something "out there" could make you feel good. Because you believed that, you looked for things to make you feel good when you felt bad. Over time, the cookie and milk could be replaced by snack food, cigarettes, alcohol, drugs, gambling, possessions, dangerous experiences, or toxic people. In other words, Grandma taught you addiction –

and it's tough to overcome because it is driven by memories from when you were six years-old.

You can make changes by challenging the things you learned from Grandma. First, you can realize that in the real world you will not always feel good. You will have bad days but realize that you will get through them without having something from "out there."

You can also decide to enjoy life by paying attention to it. Paying attention to aspects of life you enjoy is a natural way to feel good. You can enjoy your environment, people you love, good experiences, and of course the little things that make life enjoyable. That is the natural way to feel good.

FEELING SORRY FOR YOURSELF

WE ALL HAVE the natural ability to comfort ourselves when we are in emotional distress. However, we got trained out of comforting ourselves when we were told, "Quit feeling sorry for yourself." You can only comfort yourself when hurting if you can have sympathy for yourself for feeling bad.

When you were feeling bad as a child, you appealed for sympathy by whining. An adult got impatient with you because they did not know what to do to satisfy you so they told you to "quit feeling sorry for yourself." You did not feel better but you decided to have no sympathy for yourself. This memory from childhood gets in the way now for you to comfort yourself. When you're feeling bad, you are stuck with that feeling, with no escape.

When you cannot escape feeling bad, you may take it out on other people unfairly. Or, you may expect others to comfort you when you cannot comfort yourself, and get angry at them for not doing so. Others are frustrated because nothing they do makes you feel better. Kind words, a good meal, a gift, a hug, encouragement, rationalizing the bad feeling, pointing out reasons for feeling good, distracting, etc. don't make a difference. Frustrating.

The way to release your ability to comfort is to decide it is okay for you to have sympathy for yourself. You can tell your subconscious, "It is okay for me to feel sorry for myself." The emotional healing can then begin.

You may fear that once you let yourself feel sorry

for yourself, you cannot stop feeling sorry for yourself. You may think that you are going to feel even worse because you let yourself feel sorry for yourself. The opposite occurs – you begin to feel better as you experience internal comfort so there is less reason to feel sorry for yourself.

If you can recall a memory from childhood when someone told you to quit feeling sorry for yourself, you can neutralize that memory. Allow yourself to remember that experience, and then tell your subconscious to forget that memory. The memory does not disappear but it will not affect you any longer.

To avoid this problem in the future for children, comfort them instead of telling them to quit feeling sorry for themselves.

FEELING GUILTY

FEELING GUILTY COMES from violating your own moral standards.

We all develop our moral standards of right and wrong from childhood. If we experienced constant correction as children, we may have impossibly high standards for ourselves as adults. We expect more from ourselves than we expect of anyone else. We cannot help but violate these excessively high personal standards so we feel guilty much of the time.

If, as children, we experienced little correction, our standards became very low. Anything we did was okay with the people around us. As adults, these low standards enable us to do bad things without the pangs of conscious. We can treat people badly, be dishonest in our transactions, or lack loyalty to the people closest to us. There is little guilt to connect us with our moral standards.

The feeling of guilt is positive when it puts us in touch with our own standards that we live by. If the feeling of guilt is excessive, that means we have unrealistic standards to live by that we cannot achieve. If the feeling of guilt is minimal, that means that we have low standards to live by.

Excessive guilt is often about other people. We feel guilty when someone else feels bad, has troubles, is angry, or complains. Our unrealistic moral standards require us to keep others from feeling bad, save them from their troubles, do things so they don't get angry, and fix life for those who complain. We will fail at these because we can't live to that standard.

Those with a low level of guilt even when they have caused someone else pain have a low moral standard of behavior for themselves. Their lives reflect this low standard with bad relationships, legal problems, distrust of others, and difficulty making life work. These people tend to be rejected by society.

The memories behind guilt can be modified through the subconscious. If you tell yourself to forget those memories that make you do right, the compulsive excesses in your memories can be neutralized. To have a good standard for yourself, tell yourself to remember those memories that let you do what is right. Your sense of guilt will become a realistic connection with your own standards.

A good rule for yourself is, "Never violate your own moral standards." This is a rule you can also pass on to others.

UNDERSTANDING OTHERS

HOW DO YOU come to understand someone else? None of us really understand others by figuring them out, by trying to put ourselves in their shoes, or by asking someone who knows the person. To see how difficult it is to enable you to understand someone else, ask someone to explain their spouse. They can tell you things about that person but they cannot enable you to understand that person. There is only one person who can enable you to understand someone, and that is the person themselves.

Our fear of closeness can keep us from learning about someone from themselves. We use various strategies that block coming to understand that person. The person tells us something they have done, and an experience they have had, or some incident that has occurred in their lives. Rather that pursing the subject further, we talk about a thought triggered in ourselves and lose the opportunity to understand the other person better.

Once a person tells you something about themselves, their lives or experiences, stay on the subject. A little period of silence may encourage the person to tell you more. Thus the first thing a person tells you may be an introduction to a number of things they can tell you that will increase your understanding of that person. Talking about your stuff does not increase your understanding of the other person.

You may be tempted to add to what the other person tells you. For example, when the person tells about a place they visited, you might say "I was there once" rather than opening the door by asking "how was it?" The first statement closes the door to learning more, the second statement opens the door to understanding more.

Relationships are built on mutual understanding. Some people might let you tell your story if you listen to their story first, and you can do that. Some people will not help you understand them even when you are willing to listen. Other people will not listen to you enough to get to know you. Your friends are those who help you understand them and who are interested in understanding you. These people are your treasure.

HOW TO HAVE COMPASSION

THERE IS AN early childhood decision that keeps a person from having compassion. The memory has to do with feeling bad. It has to do with the child feeling bad by being scolded, punished, berated, bullied, or otherwise mistreated by others. Anyone can make the child feel bad, trapping the child in a state of feeling bad. In order to have some hope in the situation, the child decides that "when I grow up, I'm not going to let anyone make me feel bad." This decision gets stored as a subconscious memory that controls adult behaviors.

The adult living from this memory is able to fight feeling bad in adult situations. Criticisms can be fought off so they do not affect the person, attacks can be shrugged off, and negative feelings by others do not matter. This behavior is self-defense coming from memories of not having a means of self-defense. It works.

The defense against letting someone make you feel bad can also rob you of the ability to be compassionate - it can keep you from feeling bad for someone else. You protect yourself from feeling bad by distracting yourself from the other person's feelings. You may try to help the other person, give them advice, or simply get away from the person. You may not visit them or call them because you will feel bad. You are living from the decision not to let anyone make you feel bad.

Compassion comes from a new decision that it is

okay to feel bad. This decision allows you to be sensitive to others who are hurting rather than trying to get away from them. After all, you are an adult - you can handle feeling bad. Tell your subconscious that it is okay to feel bad.

An additional benefit of this decision is that you can pay attention to others' feelings without fear. It allows you to connect with the people you love who you might otherwise keep at a distance.

HOW TO LOVE YOURSELF

LOVING YOURSELF IS natural. It's loving yourself that makes you provide for yourself, take care of yourself, have good friends, and to love others. Yet, it appears that many people give the appearance of not loving themselves. These are the people who turn you down if you want to do something good for them.

People learn not to love themselves. It begins at age two when someone tells the child, "Don't be selfish, share your toys." This is followed up with "Don't be selfish" when the child shows signs of loving him or herself. A feeling of guilt is associated with loving self so that it feels forbidden. As an adult, this person is compelled to consider others before he or she can go for what they want. Only when others are satisfied can this person be satisfied, and others may never be satisfied.

Love is the desire to do good for someone else or for one's self. When we love others, we feel like doing good things for them. When we love ourselves, we feel like doing good things for ourselves. What if those feelings are no longer accessible to us?

The fact is, you do still love yourself. Look at all the things you do for yourself every day in grooming yourself, maintaining your health, getting something you want, keeping yourself safe, and a multitude of other things. You do love yourself except when you think it is selfish to love yourself.

Sometimes people seem to go to extremes in loving themselves. Actually, they are not loving themselves but struggling with loving themselves. They act out of two modes: "I cannot love myself" and "I have to love myself." When they are in the "cannot love themselves" mode they are not doing what is good for themselves. When they are in the "have to love themselves" mode they become self-centered in meeting their needs. Truly loving yourself balances with loving others.

You can deal with the childhood memories by telling your subconscious to forget those memories that make you think you are selfish if you do good things for yourself. Tell yourself it is okay to do good things for yourself.

When you love yourself, others are more likely to love you. People sense how you treat yourself and will treat you likewise.

THE NATURE OF LOVE

LOVE IS THE desire to do good for someone else. It's a natural desire that comes from the instinct that makes us want to do good from childhood. As children, we welcomed the chance to do something good for our friends, teachers, parents, grandparents, playmates, or any one of many people. Expressing our love felt good.

However, love often got defined as something else by the people around us. Instead of being about doing good for someone, love became about possessing things. We heard the word "love" used in connection with loving things, clothes, favorite foods, or toys rather than in connection with doing something for someone. Adults talked about loving their car, their house, their job, their neighborhood, and many other things. Listening to them, we came to think of love as a feeling for what we possessed. Love became about things rather than people.

Subconsciously, we have carried this attitude into adult life. With this attitude, love was about what we wanted, not about what's good for someone else. Even in romance, love became more about wanting to be with that person for one's own pleasure and less about enjoying doing good for that person. Of course, being with someone is part of romance, but togetherness sours without the basic desire to do what is good for your partner. You see a good marriage when you see two people doing what is best for each other.

How do you change your attitude? It's not as difficult as it may seem. A little conversation with your self will help. Tell yourself (subconscious) to forget those memories that make you love things. Then tell your subconscious to remember those memories that let you love people. The changes will come from within, from your heart (subconscious).

The big change you may notice is that you turn from viewing people as if they were things. Your rediscovered love for people will allow you to hear their thoughts, feel their feelings, care about their situations, and make life better for them. Love does exist in our world, beginning with us.

RESPECT

WE ALL WANT respect. We want respect from our peers, certainly from those closest to us, from those who are inferiors to us, and even from strangers. We also want to have self-respect. But what is respect?

There are two concepts of respect. The first concept of respect is based on fear. It is looking up to someone, standing in awe of someone, avoiding giving offense, and being sure to be safe in the presence of someone who has power over us. This is the kind of respect we demand of others under some kind of threat. It is the kind of respect we try to induce by scaring others, especially children. If we do not get this kind of respect, we get angry.

The second kind of respect is to value someone. This kind of respect takes into consideration another's feelings, abilities, situation, desires, and other important information. This kind of respect can be extended to spouse, friends, strangers, children, and even infants. This kind of respect does not seek to scare someone but rather to value that person.

A husband gives his wife this kind of respect when he realizes that she has had a trying day. This is the kind of respect that is expressed by dealing with the person at the head of the line first. This is the kind of respect extended when giving permission to play even though it creates noise. This is the kind of respect extended to an infant by taking care of the infant.

This is the kind of respect you can extend to yourself by caring for your own needs. Always putting others first over your own needs is a lack of respect for yourself. To respect yourself, value yourself.

Valuing of children is respect that enables the child to learn respect. The child who gets respect knows how to give respect.

The nature of respect we express goes back to childhood memories. These memories can be of others forcing respect from us by intimidation or worse. To be free of them, tell yourself to forget those memories that make you respect others.

Respect in childhood that valued you as a person supports your valuing others. To reinforce those memories, tell yourself to remember those memories that let you respect others.

Relationships thrive when there is mutual respect.

LONLINESS

DO YOU FEEL lonely even when you are with other people? You may be experiencing psychological loneliness that comes from having subconsciously rejected parts of yourself. It comes from actually deciding at some point, often in childhood, that you do not want to be like someone you know. You may have decided you did not want to be like your mother, father, uncle, sibling, or cousin. It is a decision often made when you experience someone you do not like.

The parts you've rejected take on a life of their own so you find yourself behaving like the person you do not like. You get angry at yourself for behaving like that person so the split from those parts is continued. The loneliness you experience is for those parts of yourself you have rejected. You may even feel an empty spot in yourself.

To overcome the loneliness you need to decide it is okay to be like that person you don't like so your subconscious can welcome back those missing parts. To decide it is okay to be like someone does not mean you force yourself to like that person. You can continue to dislike that person because of their behavior.

You also need to decide it is okay for you to do things differently from that person you don't like. You both have two hands but you can use your hands differently from that other person. You do not need to get rid of one hand to be different from that person.

HOW TO THINK

DOES YOUR MIND go blank sometimes? Do you have to read something several times to understand it? Do you lie awake at night because you cannot stop thinking? If so, early memories are interfering with your thinking.

The early memories come from age two when you would get into trouble, and what two-year-old doesn't get into trouble? You did not like being in trouble so you tried to figure out what you did that got you into trouble. The problem in figuring it out at that age was that you could not tell the difference between thinking and doing. You thought you got into trouble because of what you thought rather than what you did. This was confirmed for you when your mother told you "do not even think about it" when you were about to do something.

You decided it was dangerous to think. This decision was stored in your subconscious where it interferes with your thinking as an adult. So, when you are put in a position of having to think, like being asked a question, your subconscious shuts down your mind to protect you from the "dangers" of thinking and your mind goes blank. When you read something that requires you to think, your subconscious protects you from the "dangers" of thinking by shutting down your mind. You have to read the same thing over and over to finally get it. But, in bed at night, when no one can see you, your subconscious decides it is safe to think and you cannot sleep because you cannot stop thinking.

How do we change that? Your subconscious needs some special instructions from you. Tell your subconscious to forget those memories that make you think because those memories don't let you think.

Fortunately, you do good thinking much of the time so you can tell your subconscious to remember those memories that let you think. After a while, you'll notice your thinking improving when you are put on the spot, your comprehension improving of what you read, and being able to comfortably sleep with your mind quieting down.

WHAT DO YOU BELIEVE

MANY YEARS AGO, I decided that if anyone could destroy my faith, I wanted them to do it. Not that I wanted my faith destroyed, I wanted it tested. If someone could destroy my faith, that would prove to me that what I had believed was not true. That decision made a listener out of me.

Faith can come from believing an authority or from analyzing the evidence. All of us do both.

We learned to rely on authority when we were about four years-old. Someone lied to us, we were devastated, ran to mother to tell her, and she chuckled, telling us that we cannot believe everything we hear. That made us wonder what we could believe. We decided that to be safe we could believe what Mom believed. She became the expert we relied on, the authority for our beliefs. Later on, Mom would be replaced by others whose authority we believed.

At times we discovered that these "experts" were not reliable. They told us things that were not entirely true but actually were their own opinions. We had to find another way to decide what to believe, so we turned to evidence. As we analyzed what evidence we had, we learned to figure things out. We became free to think. We held off on believing until we were satisfied with the evidence.

Many people become so comfortable with accepting authority as a basis for belief that they avoid doing the analysis. These people are sure of what they believe because they have it on good authority that they do no further thinking. In other words, once you believe, you stop thinking about that subject.

Analyzing the evidence puts you much closer with reality. Believing an authority puts you in touch with his or her opinion which may coincide with reality.

Analyzing evidence is a scientific approach to reality. Believing authority is a religious approach to reality. While we may do both, it is good to understand the differences between them. The better our connection with reality, the better are the possibilities for our lives.

CONTROL OVER OTHERS

AS CHILDREN WE were controlled by our parents, babysitters, older siblings, neighborhood bullies, and many others who were stronger than we were. There was little we could do but to give ourselves hope. We decided that "when I grow up I'm not going to let anyone control me." It sounded like a good decision at the time.

The problem with that decision was that it meant we had to control others to keep them from controlling us. Most of the people around us were living from the same decision so relationships became controlling contests. This is especially true at home because it was at home that we felt controlled. When two people get into an argument, they are actually trying to control each other. Controlling goes nowhere.

A change of attitude is in order. As adults, others cannot control us but they will try. Realizing that no one can control us sets us free from the controlling contest. But, we need to realize this freedom on a deeper level than just consciously. We can achieve this freedom by telling ourselves it is okay for someone to control me if they can. When others try to control us we discover by experience that they cannot control us – we can still do what we want to do.

Anger is the tool used to control others because most people are scared of anger. Someone's anger makes them cave in to control as if they are actually being controlled. To be free, we need to overcome the fear of anger.

Fear of anger is learned in the first two or three years of life when someone's anger toward us felt life threatening. Because we were scared, we looked for ways to be safe. This memory makes the adult worry about someone getting angry, thus making the adult look for a way to be safe from that anger. This fear of anger can be relieved by telling the subconscious to forget that memory that made you scared of anger as a child.

Of course, safety is an adult issue – safety from accidents, illnesses, losses, toxic people, and many other things. Energy spent on real issues of safety is better than the energy spent on the fear of someone getting angry.

FEELING FREE

AS CHILDREN, OUR freedom was limited by parents, other family members, and by those who had responsibility for us. In response to being limited, we decided that freedom was being able to do whatever we wanted to do. This becomes a memory stored in our subconscious that makes us think that we should be able to do whatever we want. The effect may be that we do not honor boundaries or that we feel the lack of freedom.

We are never able to do anything we want. There are always limitations imposed by circumstances, necessity, society, other people, and our own abilities. There are rules to follow. That does not mean that we are never free. It does mean that freedom is having choices rather than complete freedom from control.

If you have no choices, you are trapped, not free. When you start a sentence with "the only thing I can do is…." you are expressing the feeling of being not free.

If you have only two choices, you are still not free emotionally. Two choices represent a dilemma that leaves you feeling cornered, not free. Memories of parents giving you an "either do this or else" command drives this feeling of being cornered as an adult.

You feel free when you have three choices. You can help yourself feel free by figuring out what choices you have, making sure that you have at least three choices. If you feel that you have only two choices, take the time to figure out a third choice. You did this naturally as a child –

when mother gave you a choice of two outfits to wear to school, you automatically began to look for another outfit so you would have three choices.

In raising children, you can create the feeling of being free by offering three choices. Rather than saying, "Either stop doing that or go to your room" you can say, "Do that quietly, go outside, or go to your room." The child will feel the freedom that comes from having choices.

To reprogram your subconscious, tell yourself "forget those memories that make me be free" because those memories are actually of struggles to be free. And, tell your subconscious, "Remember those memories that let me be free" because those memories are of having choices.

DEALING WITH GRIEF

GRIEF IS A natural response to loss of any kind. We all experience these losses and we all grieve. Of all the losses we experience, the most difficult loss is that of a person we love. During the first days, the grief comes in waves as the person realizes something else that has been lost with the death of the loved one. The frequency of the waves of grief declines but moments of grief can happen months or even years later when the loss is felt. This grief is cleansing, allows a person to come to terms with the loss, and enables the person to get on with life.

There is grief that hangs on. This grief is always on a person's mind as the person obsesses over the loss. Fighting the feelings only makes them stronger and the person feels even more helpless. Trying to find ways to feel better doesn't work. Efforts by others to cheer the person up seem to make the person feel even worse. This kind of continual grief is especially present when a loved one is dying over time. During that time, it is hard to cope with life even if a person wants to do it.

There is a strategy for coping in spite of grief. This strategy sets aside a half-hour to grieve at a time of day when the person can be alone and reasonably certain of not being interrupted. During the half-hour, the person does what is called grief work by thinking of all the circumstances that trigger sadness. If necessary, the person repeats the process until the half-hour is up. Other sad memories can be included in this grief work.

During the day, the person puts off grief remembering there is a time set for grieving. When the time comes, it is important to do the grief work even if the person is feeling okay at the moment. The okay feeling comes from putting off the grief so it is tempting to put it off when the time comes. However, the grieving is necessary for recovery.

Relief from grieving usually comes with one or two sessions although sometimes many sessions are needed.

TEMPER

ANGER IS A natural response to injustice. If you or someone you care about is treated unfairly, it is natural to get angry. This anger is positive – it gives you focus, strength, energy, courage, determination, backbone, fearlessness, and other things that enable you to deal with the injustice. Unfortunately, even though we experience the anger, we may not be able to act on it.

It was especially during childhood when we were not allowed to get angry. We had to suffer injustice without expressing our anger at it. We could not get rid of the anger so we hid it from others and eventually from ourselves. After that, we could be treated unfairly without getting angry. We lost the ability to deal with wrongful treatment.

The hidden anger, the anger hidden from ourselves, became the source of our temper. Little things could trigger that hidden anger so that it was expressed inappropriately over minor events. We could have a tantrum about a dish being out of place, over someone forgetting to keep a promise, over not being told about something, being inadvertently left out, and many such events. If it seemed a little unfair, the anger came out all out of proportion.

On the other hand, real injustices did not trigger anger because our memories told us to hide that anger. We became something of a doormat for others.

Sometimes, the hidden anger can create real disaster, as when the person who seemed unable to hurt a fly engages in hostile behavior that can leave others dead or injured. The hidden anger got released in some way.

Self-talk can help if you do have a temper. Tell yourself it is okay to get angry so you don't have to hide your anger. Also, tell yourself it is okay to hide the anger that you don't want to express, as long as you don't hide it from yourself.

Anger is okay that enables you to deal with injustice. Emotional anger coming from past memories is not okay.

LIVING IN HOPE

WHY DO SOME people have a pessimistic view of things while others have an optimistic view? The difference goes back to an early memory when the child, having experienced disappointment, decided that he or she would not get their hopes up again. Thus, pessimism was born. Pessimism is a defense against the pain caused by disappointment. The reasoning of pessimism is that if I do not allow my hopes to get up, then I won't experience the pain of disappointment. But, the effect of the decision to suppress hope, is a life of hopelessness.

Even the joy of good things happening is tempered by thinking, "if I let my hopes up, I will be disappointed and that will hurt." So, the person is unable to enjoy even the good things that happen because of pessimism.

Hope is the major motivator that moves us toward accomplishing good things. The other major motivator is fear that makes us flee from things. Hope draws us, fear drives us. Hope gives us direction, fear gives us energy. We need both. If we give up hope, we become depressed. If we were to give up fear, we would lose our sense of safety. Fearlessness can kill.

It is more likely that a person will give up hope than give up fear. In order to hope again, a person needs to accept the possibility of the pain of disappointment. This is possible, because as adults, we have the resources to handle disappointment that we did not have as children. If you can remember an incident from childhood when you experienced disappointment, you can tell your subconscious to forget that memory to lessen your fear of disappointment.

You can also tell your subconscious that it is okay to take the chance of being disappointed, in other words, to let your hopes up. It is better to live from hopefulness than hopelessness. It certainly feels better.

NO APOLOGY NEEDED

AN APOLOGY CAN make things smoother when you bump into someone, overlook something, forget something, or otherwise inconvenience someone. Most of the time, that apology is enough to make both of you feel better.

However, sometimes an apology may actually make things worse. A cashier, new at her job, noticed that people scowled when she apologized for keeping them waiting while she called for a supervisor to correct a problem. She changed her apologies to statements of appreciation, thanking people for waiting. Scowls turned to smiles when she thanked them.

An apology is psychologically a plea that says, "Please don't be angry at me." The person may think, 'If you are so sorry, why don't you do it right so you don't have to apologize?' An apology asks the person to forgive you as well as to endure what you have done. That doesn't feel good.

On the other hand, thanking a person for waiting, understanding or for being kind, focuses on the person's good qualities, creating good feelings in place of irritation. For example, a mother made the day for her five-year-old son when she thanked him for being patient while waiting for her. For the next couple of days, this boy walked about with his chest out saying, "I am a patient boy." He felt good in spite of how he had had to wait for his mother.

Save the apologies for the little things. When you really make life difficult for someone, thank them for having patience with you. They will not only feel good about themselves, they will feel good about you. You do not need to do everything perfectly to have good relationships because you can thank people for putting up with you.

You can even turn criticism positive by telling your critic, "Thank you for being honest with me." The criticism may hurt, but you will feel good by the reaction you get when you express appreciation. Your critic will also get a new appreciation of you for recognizing good in them.

MOTHER ROLE

A MOTHER'S ROLE can be stressful. If she is a single parent, she has to do all the parenting and her role may be blurred. If she is in a stressful marriage, she may be distracted from her parental role. If she works outside the home, it becomes necessary to accomplish parenting in a limited amount of time. Even the mother who has everything going for her can find parenting stressful if her demands are too great on herself.

Mothering can become more comfortable when the mother realizes that parenting a daughter is different than parenting a son. A daughter looks at a mother differently than a son does. A daughter sees mother as a role model because she wants to grow up to be a woman. So the way mother does things, the feedback she gives to her daughter, and the correction and approval are vital to the daughter. The challenge to Mother is to be the kind of woman she hopes her daughter will become and to give guidance to her so she knows how to do things as a woman. Mother's approval is important. Daughter gets her self-confidence from her mother.

A son on the other hand, needs to know Mother likes him. He wants to become a man so does not want to grow up to be like her but craves to know what he means to her. He does not want her to tell him how to do things as much as he wants to know how she feels about the way he does things. She's his cheerleader. He is getting his self-esteem from her. How he feels about himself comes from his interaction with her.

For a single mom the challenge is to enable her daughter to have interaction with a man who likes her to enable her to have good self-esteem and her son to have contact with a man who can be a role model to give him self-confidence. The parenting job is meant to be shared.

RAISING HAPPY CHILDREN

MOST PARENTS WANT to have happy children. They like to see their children having fun with each other and their friends, laughing, enjoying themselves, and content with what they have. Many children are happy but some parents, try as they might, cannot create happiness in their children. In fact, the more they try to make their children happy the more unhappy the children become. One reason for the unhappiness is that the parents are giving the children attention for being unhappy.

Children tend to repeat the behavior for which they get attention. Parents who want their children to be happy tend to give the most intense attention to their children when they are unhappy. When the children are unhappy, the parents become motivated to do whatever they can to make the children happy. However, when the children are playing happily, parents don't want to disturb them because they don't want to interrupt their play. So the children get attention when they're being unhappy and ignored when they are happy. Unhappiness is reinforced.

Children do need attention when they are unhappy. They need comforting, reassurance, solace, and caring. This attention needs to be balanced with even more attention when they are happy. Parents who play with their happy children reinforce their happiness.

When school is out for the summer, opportunities abound for parents to play with their children. And, it's easier to parent children who are happy than children who often need attention for being unhappy.

MAKING MARRIAGE DURABLE

THE ANSWER TO a durable marriage is in the bonding that happens during courtship and during the marriage itself. The better the bond between husband and wife, the more durable, enjoyable, and satisfying the marriage.

Emotional bonding is developed by a couple during dating. A couple goes on a date, pays attention to each other, and get insights into each other. The more variety they put into their dates, the more they learn about each other as they react to the experiences they share. When they are apart, they process what they have learned about each other and bonding develops. For bonding to be effective, they need to avoid alcohol on dates because it inhibits mental processing. Bonding also tends to diminish if they live together because they do not have the alone time to process and they don't pay as much attention to each other.

It takes about a hundred dates to establish a strong bond with each other. If you did not have the hundred dates, you can still have a good marriage by continuing bonding after marriage. Bonding happens when a couple gets out of the house together at least once a week to do something both enjoy. Bonding does not happen at home because they tend to feel controlled at home just as they did as children at home. Freedom to enjoy each other promotes bonding and that freedom happens away from home.

The wedding itself is a bonding experience that makes a couple feel married. Unfortunately, drinking at the wedding keeps the couple from processing the experience so the next morning they may not feel married even though they are. Again, it is sad to lose that bonding effect but continued bonding during marriage can compensate for it.

RELATING 101: NON-VERBAL

A RELATIONSHIP IS made up of many encounters. Every encounter can have up to six elements in it, the first being the non-verbal. When two people encounter each other, whether strangers or friends, the first communication is physical. They observe each other, read their facial expressions, thus laying the foundation for the rest of the encounter.

If they read something negative in the facial expressions, the encounter is off to a poor start. It does not become a positive foundation for the encounter. On the other hand, if they get something positive in the facial expressions, they are off to a good start.

The most positive facial expression is, of course, a smile. It provides an instant warm connection. However, if the smile is not genuine, it's not good for an encounter because people do sense when a smile is not genuine. A smile could be unnatural because you do not like the person, or it may be unnatural because it is blocked by childhood memories.

During childhood, someone, like a parent, wanted you to smile and you did not feel like smiling. You were told to smile, but you either could not smile or you faked a smile. You certainly did not feel like smiling just because you were told to smile. This experience was recorded as a memory that still affects you today.

So, when you encounter someone under the influence of this memory, you may not smile or you may fake a smile. You can reprogram your subconscious by telling yourself to "forget making yourself smile."

You do have a natural smile in certain situations. You can reinforce the memories that let you smile by telling yourself, "It is okay to smile." You want this natural smile to show up as the first step in a desirable encounter.

Of course, you may not want to smile if you do not want to connect with a certain person. A real smile is good for relating to family and friends. Since a good smile connects you with people, it is also important in the work place where you want to connect with fellow workers and customers.

RELATING 101: GREETING

A GOOD RELATIONSHIP is made up of good encounters. An encounter contains up to six levels of communication, the second of which is greeting the other person. The first level of communication is the smile "I like seeing you." Next, greeting the person says, or is supposed to say, "I like you" unless the message is tainted by childhood memories.

The troubling childhood memory comes from around age four or five when you were playing with a playmate who offended you by throwing sand in your face or breaking your toy. Angry, you stomp into the house to tell your mother what he (or she) did, and scream that you don't like him (or her) any more.

Your mother wants to smooth things over so she says, "Don't say that. Of course you like your friend. You've played together for a long time. He didn't mean to do what he did." You hear the message from your mother that you are to like your friend even though at the moment you certainly cannot like your playmate. Unable to do anything else, your subconscious stores the memory that you have to like someone even though the person is unlikable.

This negative memory can come through subliminally as you greet a person. The words you use may say "I like you" but the tone of voice says "I don't like you." The person you greet like this picks up on the tainted greeting and the encounter gets derailed.

Of course, if you like the person you are greeting the tone of voice also says "I like you." The encounter grows as it should.

You can overcome the effect of being told to like your playmate by telling yourself to "forget that memory that makes you like people." That memory doesn't let you like people. On the other hand, you have memories of liking people that you can reinforce by saying to yourself, "Remember those memories that let you like people."

With your smile and friendly greeting, the foundation is laid for a good encounter that contributes to your relationship.

RELATING 101: CONVERSATION

TWO PEOPLE TALKING together is not necessarily two people having a conversation. It is often just two people taking turns talking about themselves without actually listening to each other. Conversation is when meaningful information is exchanged between two people that let them know each other better. This is the nature of conversation even if the two people have been married to each other for decades. There is always something more to learn about each other because we all keep changing.

What keeps us from being interested in the other person? We got trained out of being curious early in life, at a time when we were intensely curious. At around age four we had a thousand and one questions about what someone was doing. We asked things like, "what is this, where does this go, why do you have two of these, how come that is purple, and so on. The barrage of questions became a distraction until we were told "I don't have time to answer your questions. Go find something to do and leave me alone." Subconsciously, we learned that giving in to our curiosity would get us rejected. That memory got stored, forever making us careful about being too curious.

Here's what happens. We meet someone with whom we'd like to have a conversation. We get through the initial smile and greeting, but we run into trouble conversing. We can't think of anything to say – and maybe the other person cannot either. Neither one is able to give voice to their curiosity, so that they appear to have no real interest in each other. The memories tell us "be careful or you'll be rejected for being too curious." This prevents the conversation from developing.

In order to engage in conversation you need to indulge in your sense of curiosity about the other person. This is more than simply asking questions like, "How was your day?" In fact, it is better to make statements rather than ask questions. For example, saying, "You must have had a hard day because you look tired" shows much more interest that asking, "How was your day?"

To liberate your curiosity, you can tell your subconscious to "forget the memories that make you have to know" because those memories carry the feeling of rejection. To support conversation, tell yourself to remember those memories that let you come to know about the person you are talking with. The interest you show fires up the conversation between the two of you. Happy relating!

RELATING 101: COOPERATION

HAVING STARTED YOUR encounter with a smile, a greeting, and conversation, you are ready to engage in some activity with the person. You may arrange to meet, you may join each other for lunch, or take in an activity. Whatever activity you decide to share requires agreement so you can cooperate with each other. Disagreement stops the encounter from going on.

Childhood memories can keep you from agreeing with someone. The experience creating the memories is that of being told, "I don't want any backtalk from you." The "backtalk" is actually you disagreeing with something. "I don't want any backtalk" did not make you agree, it made you hide your disagreement. The experience became a subconscious memory that affects you in adult life.

It makes you disagree with a suggestion automatically. Feeling like you have to agree, your subconscious immediately brings to mind what you disagree with and if you state your disagreement you cannot go on. You cannot build on disagreement. You want to tell your subconscious to forget those memories that make you agree because they do not let you agree.

Fortunately, you have many experiences in which you could agree with someone to the benefit of your encounter. You could do things with that person. You could grow your encounter to go on with your relationship.

Even if you disagree with most of what the other person says, you may be able to find some point of agreement. For example, if the other person suggests going to a fast food restaurant for a hamburger you can agree that is a good idea. You can then suggest a restaurant in place of a fast food place. Starting with agreement enabled you to work out the difference. If your first response was, "I don't like fast food joints" the discussion of having lunch together gets scuttled.

It may take some ingenuity to find agreement. For instance, if a person expresses a strong political opinion that you completely disagree with, you may still find agreement by observing, "You feel very strongly about that, don't you?" You may be surprised how this bit of agreement can allow you to discuss difficult subjects. Your encounter becomes a positive addition to your relationship.

Look for opportunities to agree, and your relationships will grow.

RELATING 101: PLAYFULNESS

A RELATIONSHIP SHOULD be fun but, to be fun, the two people need to be free to be playful. Most of us have our playfulness limited by a childhood memory.

Imagine a time when you were playing as a child while your mother was working hard to get the house in order. She got frustrated as you added to the mess rather than helping her get it clean. In exasperation, she said, "Quit playing, we've got work to do." Your father might have said the same thing when he was working on something in the garage. "Quit playing, we've got work to do." When this memory is triggered, it puts a stop to your playfulness as an adult.

In fact, "Quit playing, we've got work to do" made work out to be unpleasant, the opposite of play. Originally, as a small child, work was part of the fun as the child played at working with toy tools. For the grown up, playing has to take second place to work. This is especially true at home. Before you can relax and be playful, you have to have the house clean, everything picked up, and your work done. That means you will not be as playful as you could be at home.

To set yourself free to play, tell yourself to forget that memory of being told, "Quit playing, we have work to do." Then tell yourself, "It is okay to play." Your subconscious will apply these to set you free to be playful.

You can also be more playful by getting out of the house or apartment with your partner. Getting out of the house triggers the memories of childhood when you left the house to go to the playground where you played freely. Those memories in adult life automatically trigger playfulness when you leave the house. A good rule of thumb for couples is to get out of the house together at least once a week to make life more fun.

Alcohol or drugs make a person feel like they are having fun, but the fun does not contribute to the relationship. No one recommends that couples drink together to have a good relationship because it does not work. It actually destroys relationships.

Relationships are fun when people are playmates. You might discover that work can be made into play that you enjoy doing together.

RELATING 101: CLOSENESS

YOU MAY CRAVE closeness but the harder you work at it, the more it eludes you. You give compliments, you are nice, you give gifts, you listen, you pay attention, you do what is expected of you, but nothing seems to get you that closeness you crave. You are not aware of the one factor that goes into being close with someone.

Closeness is the sixth level of communication in an encounter, following a smile, a greeting, conversation, doing something together, and playfulness. Closeness naturally follows but may be blocked by childhood memories.

Closeness, intimacy, love, and friendship all depend on your being able to be yourself with another person. You got trained out of being yourself. When you were being your rambunctious two-year-old self, you were told not to be like that. As you were being yourself growing up, you were not allowed to be yourself. You were told how to be different because people were watching you. You were asked, "Why can't you be like your cousin, why can't you behave like other kids do, or why are you such a disappointment?" It was not okay for you to be yourself. You had to be "better" than that.

Those memories can sabotage your getting close to someone. Instead of being yourself, these memories make you put on a front for the other person. The front you put up becomes a barrier to the other person relating to you so the relationship is not all that it could be.

To reprogram your subconscious, tell yourself to "forget those memories that make you be yourself" because those memories actually make you put on a front. On the other hand, you are being yourself often every day when you feel like nothing is at stake. Reinforce this behavior by telling yourself, "It is okay to be yourself."

A wonderful connection is made when two people can be themselves with each other.

CREATING A LOVING ENVIRONMENT

THE WORDS THAT you speak create the atmosphere around you because they affect the people who hear them. Your words can make the environment warm or cold, depending on what you say.

If your words are negative, you create a negative environment. One of the most common negative words is "hate." The word "hate" is used to express your feelings about things around you. You may say "I hate this weather," "I hate the news on TV," "I hate having to go to work" and so on. Saying those things creates a feeling of being hated in the people who hear them. Their thought might be, "You hate your job, then maybe you hate me too." This would be especially hard on children who take these words seriously.

If your words are positive, you create a positive environment. The most common word to create this positive environment is "love." The word "love" can be used to express your feelings about many things, such as "I love this pizza," "I love the way things are here," "I love that song," and so on. The person who hears these words gets to feeling that you also love him or her. You are seen as a loving person.

We are most likely to express our feelings at home. That's where we can create a healthy environment for our spouse and children and others who may visit.

It is very difficult to change someone who is habitually negative by challenging them. It is more productive to ignore what they say and use positive words yourself. Be the kind of person who "loves," "likes," "enjoys" and so on. You will love the world you create for yourself.

COMMITMENT PHOBIA

COMMITMENT PHOBIA IS the fear of making a decision for fear of being trapped. A person may make a purchase only to fear regret that it was the wrong decision. A person may make a promise and feel trapped by that promise. A person may resist getting married out of commitment phobia or may get married only to feel trapped in the marriage. This sometimes happens to people who decided to get married after having lived together – the relationship that was good before marriage falls apart after marriage as one or the other feels trapped.

Commitment phobia is learned in childhood, often by being told, "You made your bed, you lie in it." The child understands that once he makes a decision he is stuck with it. A better message to the child might be, "If you don't like the way you made your bed, you can remake it. You're not stuck with it."

Commitment phobia can be detrimental to relationships. Others depend on you to keep your word and you find keeping your word hard to do if you are driven by a commitment phobia.

Commitment phobia is rooted in memories of having to do something. You can relieve commitment phobia by telling yourself to "forget those memories that make you feel trapped" and "remember those memories that let you be trapped." This will help you make a commitment and accept the limits that it puts on your freedom.

Once you can make commitments and keep them, the people around you will develop confidence in you. They learn to trust you, and that is important in relationships.

LIFE PASSAGES

CHANGES OCCUR IN everyone's life at certain points called "life passages". The first of the major life passages is at about age twelve when friends become more important to the child than parents. The child begins to relate to friends more than parents and develops the necessary social skills for life. If the freedom to relate to friends is stifled between ages 12 and 14, the child may not develop the skills he or she needs in adult life.

The next passage is at age 16, when the child begins to feel independent. The teenager does not want to be told what to do and how to do it because the teenager has ideas of his or her own. The child is ready to develop skills in negotiating with parents, skills that can carry on to adult life. If parents or caretakers refuse to negotiate but demand obedience instead, the child becomes a rebel or becomes unable to pursue his or her own ideas.

The next life passage occurs at age 26 when the person grows up psychologically. The change can be observed occurring in the six months before the 26th birthday. The child, now an adult, goes through an emotional turbulence. The turbulence is between dependency on others and taking on responsibility for themselves. An unhealthy marriage, in which the person is dependent on the spouse, often breaks up after age 26 as the person takes on responsibility for him or herself.

The next life passage occurs at age 38 to 42 and is called the midlife transition. Everyone goes through it, but men and women go through it differently. The transition for men is from being goal oriented to valuing relationships as well as being goal oriented. The transition for women is from being relationship oriented to valuing goals as well as relationships. You can see this difference as you observe older men relating to each other at the coffee shop while the older women are working on projects at home.

The fifth life passage happens at age 48 to 52, when the person, man or woman, reassesses their life. If they are satisfied with how life is going they continue doing what they're doing. If they find their lives to be deficient in some way, they will make changes to improve their lives.

These life changes are not optional. They are natural phases that happen outside of our control, or of someone else's control. Knowing these life passages allows us to understand each other and ourselves through life.

LIFE PASSAGE AT 12

CHILDREN EXPERIENCE A change in personality between the ages of 12 and 14 in that friends become more important than parents. They feel compelled to relate to friends because they are developing social skills that will serve them the rest of their lives. The social skills they develop will determine how they relate to a life partner, how they get along with people at work, and how they develop friendships. These years are important to a child's future.

These years can be difficult for parents of children who compulsively relate to other children constantly. This is a time when children stop sharing everything with their parents that they learn from friends. If parents are successful in limiting these contacts with friends to a great extent, the child fails to develop the social skills they're going to need. At the same time, parents need to keep their children safe. It's a tough balancing act.

In school, these middle school age children become a challenge to schools and teachers as they socialize compulsively. Middle Schools often require firm regimentation to keep the children on task.

Children aged 12 -14 who enjoy a rich developing social life are preparing to get along with people the rest of their lives. The better parents understand the children's need to socialize, the better they can parent during those years.

GROWING UP TOO SOON

IF YOU HAD the experience of having to grow up too soon, you may be stuck with a continuing sense of not being grown up. You were not ready to behave as an adult in childhood. But your concept of being an adult was set at whatever age you were, let's say eight. From then on, when you thought of being grown up, it was the eight-year-old concept of maturity.

Of course, you continued to grow up. Life experiences caused you to mature normally. For example, when you were twenty-one you had the maturity of a twenty-one year old, and at thirty you had the maturity of a thirty-year-old. However, in certain circumstances, your eight-year-old maturity took over so that you behaved like an eight-year-old rather than the age you were. Others might see you as a person who has never grown up even though most of the time you act grownup.

The eight-year-old maturity may not allow you to take responsibility, do what is necessary to make things work, express emotions appropriately, or to exercise self-discipline. Instead, in that state of maturity you can express lots of anger, blame others for the way you feel, throw tantrums, play victim, and demand that others make sacrifices you are unwilling to make. You may be ashamed of your behavior but find it impossible to stop because it is driven by memories.

To set yourself free, recall the experience where you had to take on adult responsibilities as a child. See what you saw then, hear what you heard then, and feel what you felt then. Having recalled that memory, tell your subconscious to forget that memory. If any part of that memory still seems strong, tell your subconscious to forget that part of the memory. Having neutralized the memory, it will stop being a driving force. You can choose to behave from your adult maturity without the extremes of childlike behavior.

Others will feel safer with you when they can rely on your being mature in difficult circumstances. Your relationships with family, friends, fellow workers, and even strangers will improve. You'll have the pleasure of closer relationships with people you care about.

CREATING A REMINDER

HOW OFTEN HAVE you tried to create a reminder in your mind so you remember to do something at a particular time only to have it fail? When it comes time to remember, all you remember is that you were supposed to remember something but you can't remember what it was.

There is a way to build in a reminder that works by using the word "forget" rather than "remember". You tell yourself "When I open the door to leave I will forget to take my umbrella." When you open the door you automatically remember the umbrella.

The key to this strategy is to use an anchor for the reminder. It can be something that you are naturally going to do, like open the door, put on your jacket, start the car, put your shoes on, pour yourself some coffee, or let the dog out. You picture the anchor, and then tell yourself that you will forget to make the phone call, put out the garbage, mail the bills or whatever else you want to remember. Psychologically this works because in order to forget you have to remember.

This works when you want to remember to tell someone something when you next see them. You picture that person in your mind and tell yourself, "When I see her I will forget to tell her about what happened to John." The thought will come to mind to tell her when you see her. Remembering is easy when you tell yourself to forget.

THE OPPORTUNITY OF BOREDOM

IN CHILDHOOD, BOREDOM is time when you have nothing to do and no one around to play with. Boredom is an unpleasant feeling in childhood because you want to be doing things usually with someone else. Often, to keep the child from complaining, the parent will give them something to entertain the child, like television.

These unpleasant childhood memories keep the adult from appreciating the real opportunity that comes with boredom. Boredom is the opportunity to think. It's a time when insights come from the subconscious, when creativity comes to the surface, and when life becomes interesting. Sometimes we have to give ourselves the chance to be bored so that thinking can happen.

When we feel boredom to be unpleasant, we do things to do away with the boredom. We may fill our spare time with entertainment that does not allow us time to think. We may use alcohol or mood altering substances to do away with boredom and consequently, the time to think. We may keep so busy that there is no time to think.

Rather than fight boredom, it is better to welcome it. Your subconscious will appreciate it and reward you for it. You may be surprised how satisfying life is when boredom is the doorway to our subconscious. Some people go out of their way to find time to be bored. Many successful people do just that because it contributes to their success.

One way to make good use of the time to think is to write your thoughts down on paper, type them out on the computer, or keep a journal. All of these slow down your thinking so that it is more like walking than speeding by in a car. You get to see a lot more.

You can make good use of boredom if you decide to enjoy it. You can help this along by telling yourself (your subconscious) it is okay to enjoy being bored. Even more effective might be to tell yourself it is okay to enjoy having time with nothing to do.

TRUST

TRUST IS OFTEN an issue in a marriage in which one partner has been unfaithful. The other person says, "I cannot trust you now. You have to earn my trust."

This sounds logical but it is a misunderstanding of what trust means. Trust is not something earned, it is a decision a person makes to take the risk that you are reliable. For example, if someone says "give me five dollars and I'll get us sundaes from the Dairy Queen" you are likely to trust the person to do it because the risk is not great. If the person fails to bring the sundaes and keeps your money, it is a loss you can absorb. You can afford to trust that person. If on the other hand, the person says "give me a thousand dollars and I'll double the money for you in an investment" you may not trust the person because the risk is higher than what you want to absorb.

Trusting someone means taking the risk that the other person can be relied upon. For the person whose spouse was unfaithful, the question is not whether you can keep him or her from doing it again, but rather, do I want to take the risk? The risk may be minimized by getting some help so that the betrayal does not happen again.

Often the person who does the betraying promises it will not happen again. We may choose to trust by believing that promise but we are still taking the risk that the promise can be broken.

For life to work, we have to trust people and we do it all of the time. We trust the people who serve us, our friends, co-workers, doctors, dentist, stock broker, pizza delivery person, the members of our family, etc. We take risks trusting that others will not let us down.

If you choose to trust no one, you withdraw from contact with people. To live, we must trust others. But trust is not absolute, it has limits. You decide to what extent you will trust someone. Demanding that they earn your trust is an attempt to control them.

RELIGION IN LIFE

THERE ARE TWO approaches to religion in life. One is to use religion to make life be good, and the other is to serve the world.

Using religion to make life be good is to use God to serve you by praying, doing good, or some other way to influence God to make your life good. Often, things go wrong in life despite all you have done to influence God, making you feel shortchanged and angry at God for not making life better. Or, you might try that much harder to influence God like adopting a different religion or declaring that you no longer believe in God.

Using God to make life better does not make sense. Think of all the people around the world that are much worse off than you are. Should God be making your life better while neglecting all those other people who are just as important to Him as you are?

On the other hand, you can also use religion to make life better for others. You can decide that you were put into the world to serve rather than to be served. God becomes your enabler to make life better for others rather than being your servant to make life better for you. You'll find that life makes a lot more sense that way.

There is religion that promises to make life better for you. Some of the largest churches have precisely this message and attract a lot of people who want to make their lives better. However, there is also religion that calls people to serve others in a multitude of ways. It makes for a much more satisfying life.

One does not need to subscribe to any religion to want to make the world a better place to be. You can just decide that at the end of your life you want to be able to say that you helped make the world a better place to be.

THE DRAMA TRIANGLE

THE DRAMA TRIANGLE is a useful tool for understanding the dynamics of problem relationships. It is movement within the triangle that creates the drama.

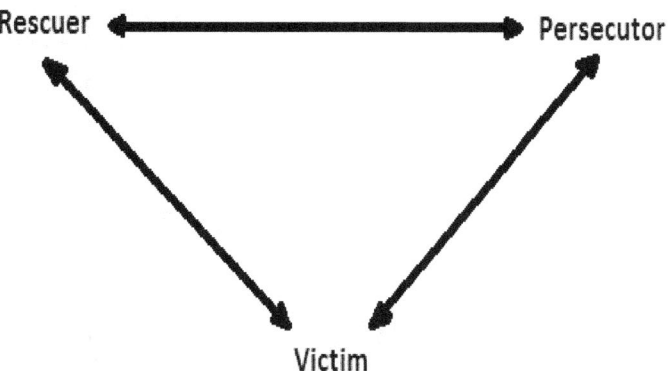

Following are problem relationships interpreted by the Drama Triangle.

Argument: This is a struggle between two people who are trying to avoid becoming the victim. Each persecutes the other to avoid the victim role. It is a contest between two people to be the better persecutor.

Punishment: This is when the persecutor is punishing someone to put them in the victim role.

Enabling: The person who enables the victim to be a victim is operating from the rescuer role. In a parenting situation, the parent does things for the child that the child is able to do for him or herself, thus teaching the child to adopt the victim role. The other parent may persecute that parent to rescue the child from learning to feel helpless or persecute the child for playing victim. The parents may then engage in a persecuting contest with each other, especially if the rescuing parent tries to rescue the child by attacking the persecuting parent.

Playing victim: The person who plays victim looks for others to rescue him or her, but fearful that others will persecute rather than rescue. For example, the problem drinker may want others to help financially but not to get him to stop drinking. When the rescuer does not save the victim, the victim may persecute the rescuer, trying to make the rescuer into a victim.

Good relationships occur outside the Drama Triangle. To get outside of the triangle, depend on yourself rather than on others to save you. Rather than rescue others, affirm their strengths with "you can do it." Don't force others to do what is right, let them take responsibility for themselves. If you say anything, tell them, "You know what the right thing to do is."

MIDLIFE CRISIS

A COUPLE MARRIED for 15-20 years, suddenly develops marital problems. One of them has an affair with a co-worker or a neighbor that they try to keep secret until their spouse finds out about it. The one having the affair is reluctant to give up the affair but also does not want to lose the marriage. This person is having a midlife crisis.

What causes a person to have the midlife crisis? Has the marriage gone stale, is the other person more attractive, or is it just that time of life? None of these causes the midlife crisis. The crisis comes from an unresolved memory of a previous love that ended with being painfully rejected. To avoid future pain, the person decides to never let anyone hurt him or her like that again.

To keep from being hurt, the person subconsciously keeps from getting close to another person. In the marriage, everything may appear healthy, but the person is not allowing the emotional closeness that would make it healthy. He or she is keeping the other person at some distance emotionally. This person does not experience the closeness in marriage that he or she experienced in the first relationship.

After about fifteen years of this kind of relating, the person discovers closeness with someone familiar, quite often a co-worker, and it brings back the great feelings from the previous relationship before the rejection. This victim of the midlife crisis is now on a high never felt before, but it is an artificial high. It comes from memories, not from the relationship.

To prevent a midlife crisis, tell your subconscious to forget that painful memory of being rejected. Also, tell your subconscious to forget that decision of not letting anyone "hurt you like that again," so you can have closeness with your partner. Love is possible when you accept the risk of being rejected so that you can be close.

A midlife crisis will pass naturally, but it may take months. If your spouse is having the crisis, time is on your side. You will need patience.

LEARNING FROM MISTAKES

"YOU LEARN FROM your mistakes" was something people told you when something you did went badly. That was to comfort you by telling you it was a learning experience. However, there is very little to be learned from making mistakes.

The student who makes the most mistakes is not necessarily learning the most. The people who make the most mistakes in life are not the most successful. Of course, those who make very few mistakes are the ones not doing much so they are not very successful either.

True learning does not come from the failure of mistakes but from successful endeavors that can be repeated. The success that teaches may be one's own achievement, it may be someone else's example, or it may be from someone teaching you how to succeed.

The problem comes when you make a mistake, and you will make mistakes. Rather than see the mistakes as just an event, you view it as a personal failure, something to be ashamed of, or as something to hide from. If you turn from feeling ashamed of your mistake to figuring out how to succeed you are more likely to succeed. The mistake does not define you, your success does.

People around you who are making mistakes show you what not to do. You don't need to make the mistakes yourself to learn what does not work.

It is tempting to get angry at someone making mistakes. Realize that those mistakes are made out of ignorance. If they knew better, they could do better.

Set yourself free by telling yourself, "It is okay for me to know how to do things." Your subconscious is ready to help you figure things out by drawing on the successful life experiences you have.

MEETING ANGER

WE ALL EXPERIENCE someone getting angry at us. At times there is no basis for the anger except for someone wanting to intimidate us to control us. At those times there is a strategy to defuse that anger.

You can call attention to the anger by saying things like "you look angry" or "you sound angry." This causes the person to dissociate from the anger so that it tends to fade away. Before it fades away, the person may say something like, "Damn right I'm angry!" after which the anger will start to fade.

When you say "you look angry" you signal to the person that you are not afraid of the anger because you can talk about it. If the purpose of the anger is to intimidate you, the person will realize that the anger is not working and may begin to talk reasonably with you. Or, the person may just walk away.

Anger that is challenged just gets stronger. For example, if you tell the person to quit being angry that person will likely get even more angry. If you tell a child to "stop it" the anger will probably increase. For the child, hearing you say "you sound angry" creates a good feeling of someone listening to him or her. The child is likely to calm down and tell you what he or she is angry about.

If you find it hard to say "you sound angry" to someone it may be that you are afraid of anger because of early memories. When someone got angry at you as a child, it felt life-threatening and all you could think of is how to be safe. That experience of fearing anger got stored up in your subconscious so that you feel scared in the face of another's anger. You need to tell yourself to "forget the memories that make you be safe" because those memories make you afraid of anger. On the positive side, tell yourself to "remember the memories that let you be safe" so you can handle yourself when someone is angry at you.

You have many safety issues in life that you address every day. Now that you are grown up, someone getting angry at you is not one of those issues.

TRYING HARD DOESN'T WORK

SOMETIMES IT APPEARS that children as well as adults need to be encouraged to work hard to achieve their goals. Doing things the easy way appears to get little done so it appears logical to tell people to try hard. Telling them to coast along does not seem to make sense.

However, a special meaning gets attached to "trying hard" that is not useful. For example, a child strikes out at the plate, goes back to the dugout dejected, and someone calls out, "That's okay, you at least tried hard." The person tries to encourage the child but the meaning may actually be, "It's not what you accomplish that's important, it's how much energy you put into it." There are a number of messages that would have been better.

It would be better to encourage the child to develop the skills necessary for success by saying "You will do better next time."

The negative meaning of "trying hard" is apparent in the ways that the words are used. For example, if someone says "I tried to do that," the obvious meaning is that "I failed." Likewise, if someone says, "I'm going to try to be there" you know not to expect them to be there. A better more positive statement would be, "I will do what I can to be there." They may still fail to be there but they are indicating that they will be figuring out how to be there rather than relying on sheer energy.

It is better to encourage children and others to work smart, not just hard. Working smart involves figuring out things. Trying hard means relying on energy to succeed at something that may fail since it is being done incorrectly. Energy will not compensate for ignorance when knowledge is necessary to accomplish something.

To help yourself, tell your subconscious, "It's okay to figure out how to do things." The better you understand a particular task, the easier it is to do and the less energy it takes. Knowledge is the alternative to trying hard.

HOW TO DO WHAT YOU WANT

EVER FEEL LIKE you cannot do what you want but always have to do what others want you to do? This feeling is rooted in childhood experiences of being told what to do rather than being allowed to do what you wanted to do (it might not have been safe to do what you wanted to do). You had no choice then but to do what you were told to do. You dealt with that situation by deciding that when you were grown up you were not going to allow anyone to tell you what to do.

You believed that the decision would make you free to do what you wanted to do as an adult but it hasn't worked out that way. People are still telling you what to do. You get angry at them but you still don't feel like you can do what you want to do. Why is that?

It is the nature of life that there will always be people telling you what to do. Family members may still tell you what to do, your employer who pays you tells you what to do, or anyone can choose to tell you what to do. Your childhood decision of not letting others tell you what to do makes you feel like you have to keep people from telling you what to do – lots of luck with that! You don't have that kind of control over others.

The childhood decision is not a good basis for adult behavior. People are going to do what they do. What you can do is change your reaction rather than try to control others. To change your reaction, you decide it is okay for people to tell you what to do and you can still do what you want to do. After all, you are grown up, aren't you? And sometimes, what a person tells you to do may be the right thing to do. In that case, it's good to do what you are told.

You can also tell yourself what to do. Doing what you tell yourself to do can give you self-discipline, enable you to keep your promises, and carry out plans that involve you telling yourself what to do. Doing what you tell yourself to do lets others depend on you. That can really improve important relationships for you.

TRUST YOUR FEELINGS

HAVE YOU NOTICED that when you make contact with a person, you get a feeling or feelings about that person? Hopefully, most of the time those feelings are positive but sometimes you get negative, scary feelings. There seems to be no reason for those feelings so you talk yourself out of them. That is probably a mistake.

The feelings you get about people go back to early in your life, when you were a baby in the crib. In the crib, you got to see people without their masks on. The adults who wear a mask around other adults drop that mask when they are alone with you. After all, who needs to impress an infant?

These experiences of people in the crib become permanent, subconscious memories that last with you a lifetime. They are there to give you insight into people by creating feelings. Those feelings you have about people are accurate. So, why don't we pay more attention to those feelings?

We get talked out of those feelings when we were a little older. One day we told Mom, "I don't like Uncle John. He's not a very nice man" because that was the way we felt about him. Those feelings were accurate but Mom was shocked about your words. She reacted by defending Uncle John, telling you that you should not feel this way about him. At that moment, she made you ignore your intuitive feelings, instead teaching you to talk yourself out of them.

You lost an important source of information about other people, your intuition. As negative feelings come up about people, you reject them only to find out later that the feelings were accurate. You need to once again trust those feelings as an important source of information about people around you.

To liberate your subconscious to trust those feelings, tell yourself to forget those memories of someone telling you that you should not feel bad about people. And tell yourself it is okay to trust your feelings. You'll be glad you did.

What if your feelings are wrong? They could be, so use them to figure out people rather than acting on them. That way you will figure out the right things to do.

WORRY DYNAMICS

DO YOU EVER say to yourself, "I wish I could stop worrying?" Worry carries anxiety with it, it does not accomplish anything, and it makes you feel pessimistic about things. It restricts you from doing what you want to do, it makes you overprotect people you worry about, and it stresses you emotionally. Much as you would like, you cannot turn worry off because it is driven by subconscious memories.

The major memory might be of being told, "Think of what could have happened when you did that!" Thinking back to what could have happened created the fear that is characteristic of worry. In fact, worry is actually you scaring yourself about what could happen.

Another set of memories that create worry come from being overprotected during childhood. Being overprotected gave you the impression that the world was full of scary hazards where you would have trouble taking care of yourself. Being overprotected made it appear to you that there really was something out there to fear. This memory taught you to scare yourself about unseen dangers "out there."

Yet another set of memories could come from a parent or other family member who was a worrier. Watching this person taught you that there were fearful things out there.

Childhood memories make you worry emotionally as an adult. This worry is very difficult to stop or to overcome. The alternative to worry is to accept that there are hazards in the world, and do what you can to mitigate them.

On the other hand, worry can be highly beneficial if it gives you a "heads up" about some danger ahead. Worry about what is over the hill when driving may cause you to slow down to be safe. It's okay for worry to encourage you to be safe.

To take the energy out of worry on a subconscious level, tell your subconscious to "forget those memories that make you scare yourself." To use your worry for safety tell your subconscious to "remember those memories that let you scare yourself." This balance can make worry useful, rather than painful, for you.

IMPORTANT VS. SPECIAL

WHICH WOULD YOU rather be, special or important? Your first answer may be special because if feels better than being important.

The difference between the two is that when you are special someone else serves you and when you are important you serve someone else.

You are being special when you are in the classroom with your teacher serving you, you are special when you visit the doctor because he or she is serving you, and you are special when it is your birthday and others are throwing a party for you. You are being important when you take care of your children, when you do something for your spouse, or when you are doing a day's work to earn a salary.

It is important to know the difference between special and important and to know when they apply. A marriage is out of balance if one person is always special and the other is always important. A balanced relationship means that most of the time they are both important to each other and once in a while one or the other is special.

Children grow up feeling special rather than important if the parents always take care of them and never ask anything of them. These children do not grow up to engage in a balanced relationship. Rather, they grow up demanding things from their partners, blaming the other person for not getting things done, feeling shortchanged, and failing to appreciate the other person.

Those who grow up being important all the time because parents made constant demands on them, see themselves as being important in a relationship. They constantly serve their partners, and seldom ask for anything for themselves.

You can make life good for yourself if you strike a balance between being special and being important. In other words, you make life good when you can receive and give love.

MOTIVATORS

YOU HAVE MULTIPLE reasons for anything significant that you do. Recognizing these reasons can enable you to think through what are going to do or to analyze why you did what you did. It pays to make a list of all the reasons you have for doing something before you decide to do it.

For example, take perhaps the most significant decision you will make in your life – getting married. The multiple reasons for getting married, besides love, can be emotional security marriage gives, respect from family and friends, assurance of being with the person you love, access to sex on a regular basis, giving your children a home environment, financial stability, escape from the dating scene, or to establish a home. Other less acknowledged reasons for getting married are an unwanted pregnancy, to escape from home, to keep the relationship from breaking up, parents push for it, and fear of losing the other person.

When you examine your multiple motivators you can judge when the action you are about to take is a good, rational and reasonable decision. You may decide it is or you may back off from the action.

You can use this kind of analysis regarding going to college, taking a job, moving to another part of the country, the kind of vehicle you want to buy, what you tolerate from a friend, how you use your money, and other decisions. This kind of analysis can save you a lot of grief. Remember, you have at least eight reasons for doing significant things that you do.

SAFETY

ACCORDING TO ABRAHAM Maslow, safety is the second most important issue in life with only survival being more important. Dealing with safety issues causes many problems people experience because people draw from childhood memories to define what is dangerous and the strategies to deal with that perceived danger. During childhood, the greatest threat appears to be other people and the strategies include hiding, placating, and getting angry with the other person. In contrast, adulthood threats are in the areas of health, finances, property, careers, welfare of family and friends, and education. Except in special situations, other people do not constitute the threat they did during childhood.

These are the childhood strategies for being safe that can be carried into adulthood:

1   Hiding – Children especially use hiding to feel safe if faced with anger from other family members. The hiding is often physical but it can also be mental or emotional withdrawal. Shyness is an expression of hiding in order to be safe. Public speaking can be terrifying to someone whose childhood safety strategy was to hide.

2   Pleasing others – Children can resort to pleasing others if they are faced with criticism frequently within the family. On those occasions when

pleasing others worked, it was reinforced as a strategy for feeling safe.

3   Anger – Children can use anger to achieve safety. However, it takes a full commitment to anger for it to work for the small child, and it does work. A full grown adult feels defeated when a two-year-old goes into a rage – you've seen it in the grocery store!

Each of the Birth Orders develops its own way to be safe. The Only's childhood strategies to be safe focus on withdrawing into one's own world, with some of pleasing others and usually very little of trying to intimidate others. This may cause the adult Only to focus on things trivial rather than on what is essential to be safe. For example, one woman cleaned house instead of getting a college assignment done. In her subconscious, she was taking care of someone who might be offended at her unclean house while ignoring the real threat posed by not getting her assignment done.

Because the First Born dealt with adults during childhood, his or her safety strategy was to satisfy these adults rather than using withdrawal or anger which were ineffective. In adult life, the First Born tends to tune in to others' attitudes to know how to satisfy them to avoid the risk of offending them. In the process, the First Born may neglect important issues in his or her own life while taking care so others are not a danger. For example, the First Born student may go out with friends to satisfy them rather than stay home to do an assignment. The First Born may buy a car beyond his means to impress a co-worker without considering the restraints of his own budget.

The Second Born childhood strategy for being safe involves withdrawal as they focus on details more than trying to please others or relying on anger to feel safe. By pursuing this strategy in adult life, they may relate poorly to others which can prove detrimental if they are put in charge of others. This is significant because focusing on details enables Second Borns to do impressive work that in turn earns them promotions that often involve supervising others. In those situations, childhood memories can make Second Borns feel vulnerable so that they use anger to feel safe especially since they cannot feel safe by escaping into detail work.

The Third Born childhood strategy may be to ignore safety altogether to become risk takers. As a child, the Third Born cannot escape the teasing of the Second Born so learns to ignore it or, in other words, regard it as a non-threat. With this attitude, they do not need to use the strategies of hiding or getting angry to feel safe. However, the memories of being vulnerable as children often make them turn to pleasing others to make their world safer. In adult life, Third Born risk-taking may ignore real risks that may result in many kinds of unpleasant outcomes. They may, in fact, pay too high a price for pleasing others rather than paying attention to critical issues in their lives. On the other hand, their risk-taking wisely done can lead to great success in life.

The Fourth Born childhood strategy to be safe involves either anger or hiding, often both. Pleasing others does not seem like an option if the Fourth Born is ignored by members of the family, as is often the case. In adult life, the Fourth Born's reliance on anger for safety may be expressed as domestic abuse, angry confrontations, and even crime. Other Fourth Born adults may seek safety in hiding, maintaining a low profile, and not expressing opinions. These Fourth Borns may hide money from the spouse, lie skillfully to cover up, or put on an act instead of being themselves. Using anger and hiding as safety strategies handicaps the Fourth Born in relating to others. However, Fourth Borns have the potential of relating well because their understanding of others grew out of being the underdog in the family - if he or she can deal with adult issues rather than fearing others.

To move on to loving relationships, self-esteem, and self-actualization in Maslow's pyramid, it is necessary to resolve the issue of safety. It is important for the adult to recognize that the attitudes of other people do not constitute a real threat so that energy can be used for resolving the real issues of adult life.

SHORT TERM MEMORY LOSS

YOUR SHORT TERM memory loss may just be that you are not paying attention. You can only remember that to which you pay attention.

You pay attention to what you see, hear, and feel. Obstruction to paying attention goes back to childhood memories with unintended consequences.

You were expected to see things as a child. You were asked, "Can't you see it? It's right in front of you!" You came to expect to see things in a particular way that did not let you see things as they are. A man could not find his gas can in the garage because it was lying on its side – he expected to see it standing up. To overcome this type of obstacle to seeing, say to yourself, "Forget the memories that make me expect to see." You'll remember new things that you don't expect to see because you are paying attention.

You were expected to hear things as a child. You were asked, "Can't you hear what I'm telling you? Pay attention!" You learned to expect to hear things in a particular way, expectations that kept you from hearing something expressed differently now. To reprogram your subconscious to hear, say to yourself, "Forget those memories that make you expect to hear" so you can hear new things. Hearing new things, you will tend to remember them.

As a child, you were expected to feel a particular way. When you didn't feel the way they expected, you were told, "Don't feel that way." Being told to feel differently than you did, created memories that interfere with you paying attention to your feelings as an adult. If you can't pay attention, you can't remember. To resolve this issue, tell your subconscious to forget those memories that make you feel. When you are free to feel, you are free to remember.

You can also tell your subconscious to remember those memories that let you see, hear, and feel.

As you pay attention to what you see, hear, and feel, your short term memory improves. You may not remember everything, but you will probably discover that your mind is okay.

SLEEP DISORDER

DO YOU HAVE trouble going to sleep, waking up during the night and have trouble getting back to sleep, tossing and turning during the night, and wake up tired in the morning and feel stiff? You may be suffering a sleep disorder caused by memories from when you were about eight years old.

The problem started when you were told to go to sleep but you were not ready to sleep. Your body said "no" because you were still energized. Other children were having fun, the sun was still shining, no one else was going to bed but you had to go to bed and you had to sleep. This experience created a conflict of memories that interfere with sleep now in your adult life. One set of memories says, "I have to sleep" and another set of memories says, "I cannot sleep."

When you go to bed, the "I cannot sleep" memories keep you awake. You may have tried to silence this memory by staying up late enough so that you are tired enough to go to sleep. Even then, you may have trouble going to sleep.

When you do get to sleep, the "I cannot sleep" memories can kick in to wake you up. Even if they don't wake you, the memories can be in conflict subconsciously during the night, causing your muscles to tense. The tension creates discomfort, making you try to get into a comfortable position. It is this search for comfort that causes the tossing and turning.

In the morning, you wake up tired because you have

not slept that well. Your body feels stiff because your muscles were made tense by the memories in conflict. During the day, you continue to feel sleepy because you did not get enough restorative sleep.

To overcome the sleep disorder, tell your subconscious to "forget those memories that make me sleep," memories of someone telling you to sleep. This message to your subconscious resolves the conflict that drives the sleep disorder.

You can improve your chances of a good nice sleep by remembering a time when you slept well. You went to sleep naturally, you slept comfortably without tossing and turning, and you woke up refreshed. Tell your subconscious to "remember that memory" so that you can sleep that way again.

SPONTANEOUS REMISSION OF CANCER

A FEW YEARS ago, a woman that I was counseling by phone asked if there were something she could say that would be positive for her father who was in hospice, dying of cancer. She wanted to make his last moments as pleasant as possible in his circumstances. I suggested she tell him, "Never get so interested in cancer that you forget to live."

When she told him that, he responded by saying "it's too late for that." However, he started getting better and in a few days he went back home to live a normal life. I think those words produced a spontaneous remission of cancer.

I've had three other instances those words caused a remission of cancer. One was a friend who was in the hospital running a fever with nodal cancer. When I walked in, I immediately said to him, "Never get so interested in cancer that you forget to live." He made no response, and we went on to talk about other things. In five days, the doctors told him his cancer was gone, and it has not returned.

Another friend, a truck driver, had colorectal cancer. We were talking on the telephone when he told me of the diagnosis. When I heard it, I told him to "never get so interested in cancer that you forget to live." He is cancer free now, a couple of years later.

I do not know why this statement works. It is a type of statement that I use in bringing about psychological change with clients. To help the man in hospice care, I adapted this statement to cancer with the results I have mentioned.

Interestingly, none of the persons I have mentioned have ever talked about what happened with their cancer. Perhaps the therapy made them lose interest in cancer so that they no longer think about it nor do they talk about it.

In helping someone, it is important to use the exact wording: "Never get so interested in cancer that you forget to live."

DIABETES

SEVERAL YEARS AGO, I counseled an eleven-year-old girl who had a severe case of diabetes. Her situation was that her parents were in conflict and took much of their unhappiness out on her. She concluded that she was not being sweet enough for her parents to be happy with her. Getting her story gave me a clue to the possible psychological connection between diabetes and not being able to be psychologically sweet enough at an early age.

I saw an extreme example of this with a middle aged man who had severe diabetes. He said his blood sugar level ran at about 400. He told me that when he was about four and a half years old his parents were both killed in a tragic car accident. His conclusion at that age was that if he had been sweet enough his parents would not have been killed. I worked with him to neutralize that memory after explaining its connection with diabetes. The next morning he told me that the therapy had worked almost too well – his blood sugar had dropped from 400 to 75 overnight!

In another case, a woman told me that her diabetes was so bad in its effects on her that her doctor was talking about amputating a couple of toes. At my urging, she recalled a memory in which she felt she was not being sweet enough to satisfy a parent. We neutralized that memory and I did not see her again for three months. When I did see her, she still had her toes and she had her diabetes under control

The memories are neutralized by telling yourself, "I

want my subconscious to forget that memory so it no longer affects me in any way." The therapy can be reinforced by telling yourself, "Forget those memories that make you be sweet" and "remember those memories that let you be sweet."

When you remember the memory behind diabetes, you can also tell your subconscious to "deal with that memory." This will have the same effect of neutralizing the memory behind diabetes.

ENJOYING SEX

WHAT IS IT about sex that gets people into trouble? Pursuing sexual pleasure destroys careers, relationships, and reputations. Why would someone jeopardize all that is important for the momentary pleasure of sex?

Attitudes toward sex are programmed into us in our childhood. Girls are programmed into not enjoying sex for fear of the consequences of girls having sex. While this programming is done by those who want to protect girls, boys are programmed by their peers. The conversation of boys going through puberty often centers on sex, either bragging or lying about sexual exploits or imagining what they want to do sexually. A lot of it is fantasy but it conveys the clear message that boys are supposed to enjoy sex. The difference between the programming for girls and boys is the difference between the words "slut" and "stud".

Fortunately, this programming is balanced out in most people with values that boys and girls learn from parents, mentors, religious teaching, peers, and their own insights. One does not have to give in to the unhealthy programming from childhood.

Women who live out their programming cannot enjoy sex. Yet, they learn from society that they must enjoy sex, and they certainly hear it from the guys who want sex. Women who live out their programming either get turned off to sex or perform sexually as a service to the man rather than for their own enjoyment. Some may even convince themselves they do enjoy sex while they try to make themselves enjoy it.

Guys who live out their programming think they must enjoy sex. Sex is an end in itself. The woman with whom they have sex is irrelevant. They can have sex with multiple partners, strangers, casual acquaintances, and prostitutes because they are not relating to the woman with whom they are seeking the pleasure of sex. For these men, sex exists apart from relationship. This can happen within marriage as well which women recognize when they complain, "He's only interested in one thing." Men may deny the accusation but the way they do sex without relating confirms what the wife says.

To achieve balance, values need to change. A woman needs to decide it is okay to enjoy sex so she can enjoy both her partner and the sexual experience. This allows her to make sex part of the relationship.

A man needs to decide it is okay to enjoy the woman with whom he is having sex so that sex becomes a way of relating rather than of exploiting her. Once these values are embraced men and women can find themselves enjoying each other in many ways including sexually.

Birth Order can be helpful as the couple explore each other's personalities as well as enjoying sex. Birth Order gives clues to personality that lead to learning from each other. Birth Order lets the couple ask the right questions, recognize what is important, and interpret each other correctly. As they come to understand each other, he'll enjoy her while having sex and she'll enjoy him while having sex. When they enjoy each other, having sex becomes making love.

Enjoying sexual relationships is the alternative to addiction. Sexual addiction is like any other addiction in that it is accompanied with feelings that sexual contact is necessary for feeling good. Sexual addiction can be so compulsive that the addict throws caution to the winds in the pursuit of sex. Meanwhile, the addict loses the possibility of real joy of sex within a relationship.

THE STRESS OF JUNE

JUNE IS THE nicest month of the year. Temperatures are neither too hot nor too cold, lots of flowers, trees and shrubs are blooming, and the insects have not yet multiplied. It's a time for picnics, ball games, fishing, bicycling, and other happy outdoor activities. It would seem the ideal time of the year and it is but for many it is a time of stress.

The stress comes from the long, hard winter when many of us looked forward to summer when life would be entirely different. We thought about all we could do when summer came. We planned reunions, trips, family activities, encouraged the children to take part in summer activities, as well as gardening, camping, and swimming. We thought summer but actually we were thinking of June. When July 4th comes, it's not the same – it feels like summer's almost gone. Summer means June.

June is only thirty days and has only four weekends. There is not enough time to squeeze in all that we dreamed of doing. Not only that, weather can interfere with plans, the SUV breaks down, Junior breaks an arm, and the summer plans are kaput. So, instead of a happy month that made up for all we had to put up with last winter, we had a month of frustration. That is stress aggravated by the fact that it will be eleven more months before June comes around again. For that reason, July is often a busy month for counseling.

By understanding that June cannot fulfill all our

dreams, we can plan more realistically. We can decide what is most important to us, what things we can let go, and enjoy the beauty that is June.

IMPROVING TEST SCORES

SOME STUDENTS KNOW their material well but are unable to recall it during testing. After the test is over, they remember what they wished they had remembered while taking the test. Just being able to recall what they know could improve test scores. But the harder they try, the worse it gets. They need to do something else.

There are three ways of processing and storing information in our minds. We can store information by seeing it, hearing it, or feeling it. Reading stores information visually, hearing lectures stores information by sound, and hands on learning stores information by feel. All of us use all three systems to process information but we tend to favor one over the others at any given moment. This becomes an obstacle in taking a test.

If you are in the feeling mode, it is hard to access material stored visually. You need to put yourself in the visual mode right at the beginning by looking at something as if you were going to paint a picture of it. It can be any object in the room. After you do this, the answers will come more easily when you are taking the test.

If you come across a question that makes you anxious, it puts you back in the feeling mode making it hard to answer questions after that. You can restore the visual mode by examining the back of your hand for fifteen seconds before going on with the test. You will be pleased with the results.

INTRODUCTION TO BIRTH ORDER

BIRTH ORDER AS I know it, goes far beyond the oldest, middle and youngest child. It recognizes five unique personalities - the Only Child, the First, Second, Third, and Fourth Born. As we go along, you will learn about each personality. You will learn about unusual situations in which your personality is different from your place in the family.

You have a personality. It is one of these five. Get ready to get acquainted with yourself, to see through others, and to enjoy your relationships more than ever.

THINKING OUTSIDE THE BOX

TO UNDERSTAND BIRTH Order it is important to think outside the box. All of us originally were taught to think inside the box. It started when we were about five or six years old. A playmate lied to us, we were devastated, and mother or father told us "you just can't believe everything you hear." That gave us the problem of how to figure out what is true. To solve the problem, we watched to see what our parents or other adults believed and decided that's what we were going to believe. Thus we learned to believe on the basis of authority and that defines our box. Our box is made up of what we believe. We can think outside the box by choosing to question authority on the basis of evidence.

Psychiatrist Alfred Adler created the box that defines Birth Order almost a century ago. He stated that Birth Order consisted of oldest, middle and youngest child. Ever since then researchers have struggled trying to prove him right. Even today, research projects that look into Birth Order always assume that it consists of three personalities. They are still thinking inside the box.

Thinking inside the box relies on authority. Thinking outside the box relies on evidence. Almost forty years ago, I found some evidence that Birth Order consisted of five rather than three personalities. It was the discovery outside the box that opened up a new understanding of Birth Order personality. I began to see how things actually are. Since then, I have been able to add an immense amount of information to the understanding of Birth Order, information I am glad to share with you.

How can you develop the ability to think outside the box? You can do it by welcoming challenges to what you believe. I made the decision many years ago that if people could destroy my faith I wanted them to do it. I wanted to believe the truth. From that point, I stopped defending what I believe. Defending my faith had kept me inside the box. Accepting challenges to my faith gets me out of the box. It allows me to consider new evidence.

A motto that can help says, "Never get so interested in believing that you forget to think." Repeat that motto to your self. It allows you to focus on evidence.

PROFESSIONAL RESISTANCE TO BIRTH ORDER

MANY PROFESSIONALS REJECT the idea that Birth Order has any effect on personality. Counselors tend to see Birth Order as offering the client a cop-out, especially if the counselor normally functions in an adversarial relationship with clients. The counselor does not want the client to be empowered by understanding Birth Order. Academic researchers cannot identify Birth Order personality satisfactorily because they study it outside the home in the laboratory setting, the school, or the work place. People do not display their Birth Order to any great extent outside of their homes. In the mall, you cannot observe people living out their Birth Order.

Birth Order is developed in the intensely emotional home environment. When the child left home for the playground, school, or daycare where the emotional environment was much less intense, Birth Order personality was set aside. Outside the home, the child learned to socialize while setting aside their Birth Order personalities. When they went home, the Birth Order personality took control again. Home brings out the Birth Order in adults as well. Away from home, they shift to a public personality. Researchers fail when they try to discover the home personality of Birth Order by studying the public personality.

The average person discovers Birth Order more

readily than professionals because he or she compares Birth Order to experiences in the family. This observation enables laypersons to see what research-oriented professionals cannot see. I learned about Birth Order from my clients because they told me about domestic experiences.

HOW BIRTH ORDER HAPPENS

BIRTH ORDER IS not caused by how parents treat their children! It comes from interaction between siblings.

An only child develops an Only Child personality by learning how to be alone without feeling lonely. The child does this by developing an imaginary companion early in life.

A First Born starts life as an Only Child until the second child is born. It is the reaction to the loss of attention to the new baby that creates the First Born personality. This child feels like he or she lives in a world without love.

The second child competing with the First Born for attention becomes a Second Born. Since the child often loses in this competition, he or she is left with a feeling of inadequacy that drives the Second Born personality.

The third child, reacting to the Second Born's teasing, becomes a Third Born. The Third Born is driven by a feeling of having to be strong so that nothing gets to him or her.

The fourth child is rejected by the Third Born telling this child "you're not big enough, old enough, strong enough, fast enough, and you don't know enough to play with us." Reaction to this rejection drives the Fourth Born personality with a feeling of being no good.

The fifth child is ignored by the Fourth Born so that the process starts over with the fifth child being an Only Child until and unless there is another child born making this child into a First Born. In large families, there can be several sets of Birth Orders.

Once the Birth Order cycle is started, parents cannot stop it. Interaction between siblings keeps it going. Also, once set, a Birth Order personality cannot be changed.

IDENTIFYING BIRTH ORDER

IDENTIFYING A PERSON'S Birth Order can be challenging. Here's a way to enable yourself to recognize Birth Order. Select a person of each Birth Order within your family as a model. When you are figuring out someone's Birth Order compare them to the five models you have in mind.

If you select models within your family, you are most familiar with them. You have seen them act out their Birth Order. People do not readily display their Birth Order personality in public although there are exceptions.

If your family is small so that all Birth Orders are not represented, pick models among the people you work with every day. You are familiar with their personalities from constant contact so they will serve well as models.

If you have to, use friends, acquaintances, or other people you know as models. This is more difficult because you tend to know them more superficially.

Birth Order was developed at home with siblings. Outside the home, even in adulthood, Birth Order personality is not as apparent in people. Watching people at the mall is not a good way to observe Birth Order. You have to see them at home.

When you have selected your models, make sure that they are the Birth Order you think they are.

After a while you can identify Birth Order naturally without models. Then the people you encounter will teach you about Birth Order. Every day you become more conversant with Birth Order.

BIRTH ORDER VARIATIONS

THE BIRTH ORDER personality can vary from the birth order position of the child in the family for several reasons. A caretaker who helps when the second child is born, the personality of the mother, multiple births, "ghost" children, and special circumstances can determine a child's Birth Order.

A first born child is an Only Child until the second child is born. Then the first born becomes a First Born by losing attention to the new baby. If, however, mother has help for the first two or three days of bringing the new baby home so the first born does not lose attention to the baby, the first born remains an Only Child despite a small age difference between the two. If there are no more children the second one remains an Only also.

If mother is under stress when the first born is two to five years old, her birth order may determine the Birth Order of the child. What Birth Order is created depends on the sex of the first born. The most common instance is that of a Second Born mom under stress who causes a first born daughter to become Third Born or a first born son to become Second Born. A son absorbs mother's personality to become Second Born, a daughter reacts to mother's personality to become Third Born. The second sibling takes the next Birth Order personality following the First Born's personality.

This effect can also happen with a Third Born mom who can cause a First Born daughter to become Fourth

Born or a First Born son to become Third Born. This effect does not happen with the other Birth Born Mom's.

Twins usually organize themselves into consecutive Birth Order personalities without regard to which one was born first. If a family starts out with twins, they will likely be First and Second Born in personality. If they have an older sibling who becomes First Born, they take on Second and Third Born personalities.

A child who dies can count in the Birth Order. There are instances where although the oldest child died before the second child was born the second child became Second Born in personality. It's as if this child had to adjust to the invisible presence of the "ghost child."

Occasionally a Birth Order personality is created in the home of a babysitter. In one instance, a child was cared for by a woman who had two children became Third Born in response to them although she was an only child. This does not happen in day care with a number of children present.

In blended families children keep the Birth Order personalities developed in the original homes. A baby born into the blended family takes on the appropriate Birth Order personality. For example, in one blended family, the new child took on Fourth Born characteristics following the Third Born of her half-sibling.

ONLIES ARE NOT LONELIES

LOGICALLY, IT WOULD seem that Only Children would grow up lonely because they lack siblings. However, logic often fails at predicting human behavior. Being alone could mean loneliness if the child did not solve the problem. The Only Child solves the problem by creating an imaginary companion or companions. Often the imaginary companion is a doll, a pet, or even a parent playing the role assigned by the child.

The Only Child shares feelings, thoughts, and ideas with the imaginary companion and, of course, the imaginary companion always feels the same way, thinks the same way, and appreciates the same ideas as the Only Child. The imaginary companion is so real that the Only Child can play for hours without feeling lonely. In fact, the time with imaginary companions is so enjoyable that this child craves time to spend with imaginary companions. That's what's happening when the child is playing "alone" in his or her bedroom.

On a subconscious level, these attitudes carry into adult life. The Only Child craves alone time often as transition time between work and home. Arriving at home, this person wants to have some time alone before getting into family activities. Often, a long commute serves as transition time for the Only. Sometimes, Onlies like to get to work early so they can be alone for a half-hour, reading the paper, and having coffee before they start their day.

Onlies also tend to treat others as imaginary. They

think about what they are going to say rather than listening to the other person, interrupt the other person to express their own ideas, and assure the other person that "I know exactly how you feel." Two Onlies talking, take turns talking without listening to each other.

Onlies subconsciously assume that others know how they feel just as the imaginary companions always knew how they felt. In communicating, they may not say what they mean because they expect others to fill in the meaning. For example, "time management" is an Only term which assumes that you understand the meaning to be "activity management" because you cannot really manage time.

Onlies like to be among familiar things that feel like friends to them. They may hang on to a previous vehicle rather than trade it in because it would be like losing a friend. If anything in their familiar environment is moved or removed, they tend to notice it immediately because when they enter their environment they make touch with their "friends" that are the things around them.

THE EMOTIONAL ONLY CHILD

THE ONLY CHILD learns early to deal with difficult situations with emotion. Imagine the two-year-old Only on the floor playing with blocks, getting frustrated because they don't work right. Someone watching wants to help the Only to get them piled right. The Only does not want the intrusion, wants to figure it out, and asks the person to not touch anything. But the adult is eager to help until the Only has to scream, flail her arms, and express her anger. With that, the adult backs off. The child has learned to get things done with emotion.

The Only Child has learned to think with feelings. In the adult Only Child, this comes out in remarks such as "I'm not comfortable with that" or "I don't know what I want to do Saturday night because I don't how I'm going to feel." "Never" and "Always" statements are an Only Child expression of emotion as in "You never help me around the house" or "You are always wanting me to do things I don't want to do."

When positive, Only Child emotion can be enjoyed by others. For example, others enjoy it when the Only emotes saying "I just love that outfit." The Only Child laugh can be contagious in a group. The Only Child smile can really make others feel liked.

To put emotions into balance, we can tell the Only "Never get so interested in feelings that you forget to think." This enables the subconscious mind to balance emotion with thought.

FIRST BORNS ARE MADE, NOT BORN

THE OLDEST CHILD is not born as a First Born but as an Only. When this Only Child gets a sibling, he or she turns into a First Born with an entirely different personality from the Only.

The oldest child is living life as an Only until one day mother brings home a tiny stranger out of nowhere. When this tiny stranger cries, mother sets the other child on the couch, tells the child to wait because she has to take care of the baby, and promises to come back soon. This child sits on the couch and waits, something he (or she) has never had to do before. The wait is interminable. Meanwhile, mother is having entirely too much fun with this stranger, cooing, laughing, and talking affectionately to the stranger. The oldest child, as an Only, used to get attention whenever they craved it. Now, suddenly, mother's love is not available on demand.

The Only Child becomes a First Born. Sitting on the couch watching Mom's back at the bassinet, the child begins to wonder what he did to lose mother's attention. The child decides it must have been something just awful for mother to reject him completely. The child doesn't know what it could be but feels guilty nevertheless. He must have done something drastic to make mother stop loving him.

The Only has become a First Born. His world is

now a world without love, love that he must get back some way. This becomes the First Born's subconscious goal. As an adult, he is going to be careful that what he says will offend no one, saying "I don't know" whenever he is not sure how something will be taken. He is going to try to get respect, admiration, and approval as forms of love he can earn. No longer will he be an Only enjoying a private world with imaginary friends but a First Born, highly tuned to what others expect in order to satisfy them.

If it happens that the oldest child is old enough, usually age five or older, to realize that mother is not rejecting him, he will remain an Only. If grandmother comes in to give the oldest child attention while mother is caring for the baby for the first two or three days so that this child gets used to the baby, the oldest child remains an Only as well. He does not experience the sudden shock of losing mother's love but rather simply having to adjust to sharing mother's love with his little sibling.

The First Born lives with free floating guilt, constant inner pressure to satisfy others, fear of being assertive lest he offend someone, and always on guard lest he lose someone's esteem. Being corrected can cause pain for days as he beats up on himself for yet again doing something to lose love.

THE ARROGANT FIRST BORN

THE FIRST BORN has only younger siblings. Growing up, the First Born always knows more than his or her siblings do. As an adult, the First Born subconsciously continues to look at others as if they were younger siblings. Often, the First Born is surprised that others know what they know, can do what they can do, and have the insights they have.

This attitude limits what First Borns can learn from others. Their first reaction to being told something is to disagree. They know something that contradicts what they are being told so they must disagree as if the other person is a younger sibling who does not know what he or she is talking about.

On the other hand, First Borns have no older siblings to limit them. This allows them to be dreamers since they have no one to bring them back to reality.

By adopting the attitude that everyone knows something, he doesn't know the First Born can be receptive to others' ideas. By realizing that he is now an adult among adults rather than the older brother, he can deal with others as equals.

If you are the oldest but the above description does not fit, First Born may not be your personality. Check out Only Child. Frequently, the oldest child is an Only Child personality rather than a First Born.

THE SKEPTICAL SECOND BORN

IN CHILDHOOD, THE Second Born has to cope with a First Born who is trying to take attention away by being superior. Whatever the Second Born does, the First Born does it better. The First Born wins at every competition. And, the First Born makes the Second Born feel stupid by playing on his or her gullibility.

Out of self-defense, the Second Born turns skeptic. Throughout life, the Second Born looks suspiciously at every new idea in case someone is trying to make him or her look gullible. If there is any hint of this intent, the Second Born attacks an idea with gusto, cutting it down with impeccable logic. "Can't let someone make a fool of me again!"

Being gullible makes a person feel stupid. The opposite should be true. The person who is gullible is intelligent enough to figure out how something off-the-wall could be true. Some really intelligent people are really gullible.

Every Birth Order can experience being made to look gullible. It's the Second Borns who battle with it for a lifetime - until they realize what's going on!

A SUPER INTELLIGENT THIRD BORN

A SPECIAL BIRTH Order situation can create extraordinarily high IQ in a person. This occurs when the oldest child, a girl, is a Third Born in personality.
The first born daughter becomes Third Born because her mother, a Second Born, is stressed out when she is very young, around two years of age. Under stress, mother interacts with her child in such a way as to produce the next Birth Order personality, i.e., Third Born in the child.

Mother's stress can come from a number of sources such as marital conflict, financial distress, family crisis, substance abuse, or psychological. The stress may be increased by the birth of a second child.

The daughter's intelligence is often accompanied with a compulsion to break the rules, violate boundaries, be impulsive, and take risks. Others may describe this person as being very intelligent but lacking in common sense.

At this point we can only speculate about the dynamics that cause this phenomenon.

If the first born is a boy under the same circumstances, he takes on mother's personality to become a Second Born. We have not seen the same kind of super intelligence in him.

Birth Order sequence takes up following the oldest child. The child following the Third Born daughter will be Fourth Born. The child following the Second Born son will be a Third Born.

THE PUSHY THIRD BORN

AS A CHILD, the Third Born had to cope with Second Born teasing. There was no winning over this Second Born unless the Third Born got pushy. Then the Second Born would back off. So, with these childhood memories, the adult Third Born tends to push people rather than to reason with them.

The Third Born salesperson just won't give up. The Third Born friend just won't take "no" for an answer. The Third Born partner insists on his or her way of doing things. As a result it is hard to work with Third Borns. They tend to do things alone or leave things for others to do. It is hard to work in cooperation with others if your main strategy is to push them rather than negotiate with them.

Dr. Phil of TV fame is a pushy type Third Born. It makes for good, dramatic TV. He confronts people with their problems, pushes them to make changes, and does not stop till the person goes along. He is very good at it. He brings a lot of knowledge, experience, and wisdom to his work but his main strategy, on TV at least, is to push people into making changes.

It can be helpful for the Third Born to realize that not everyone is a Second Born with whom you cannot reason. The Third Born needs to know that he or she is not a child surrounded by Second Borns but rather an adult among adults with whom he or she can reason. It makes for better relationships with everyone.

There are exceptions, of course. Some cautious type Third Borns are exactly the opposite. They would not pressure anyone at any time.

THE FOURTH BORN ACTOR

THE FOURTH BORN is the best equipped of the Birth Orders for an acting career. The Fourth Born learns from childhood to act out different personalities. As a child, the Fourth Born is told that he or she is not big enough, old enough, fast enough, strong enough, or smart enough to play with the older siblings. The Fourth Born tends to get a negative view of self as being unacceptable.

In order to overcome not being good enough, the Fourth Born studies others to discover how to be someone else. The Fourth Born watches how others do things to emulate them. The Fourth Born gets absorbed in a dramatic TV show, studying how to be a character in the show. The Fourth Born watches every facial expression, gesture, and move, listens to every inflection, tone, and variation in the voice to copy them. This extensive study on how to be someone else, creates a talent for portraying lots of different personalities.

The Fourth Born often acts in daily life even if he or she does not become an actor. The Fourth Born can be whoever you want the Fourth Born to be. This can be positive, as in entertaining people. It can also be negative, as in winning a court battle over custody of children as many a spouse can attest. The Fourth Born can be so convincing that the spouse ends up looking bad even though the situation may be exactly the opposite. This acting talent makes the Fourth Born capable of being the ultimate con man or woman.

Pushed to the extreme where Fourth Born acting becomes compulsive can result in Multiple Personality Disorder or as it is known now, Dissociative Identity Disorder.

The acting skill of the Fourth Born can be so good that the best of us are taken in by it. They know much more about acting than the rest of us know about identifying acting.

FOURTH BORNS PLAY ROUGH

IN PLAYING WITH older siblings, the Fourth Born learned to play rough. The Fourth Born did not have to hold back because the older siblings could take it. This Birth Order plays rough in many ways in adult life as well.

Fourth Born humor is often rough, so rough that others think the Fourth Born is mean rather than funny. Fourth Borns can insult others unmercifully, tease a child till the child cries, and intimidate others with anger. Many coaches are Fourth Borns who like to be rough with their players. The Fourth Born trying to play rough can be the loudest person at a gathering using the most profanity. The Fourth Born may be a workaholic because hard work challenges the Fourth Born to be rough. The Fourth Born can be rough at home by engaging in domestic abuse when angry. Fourth Borns can be rough with themselves by ignoring major health concerns with behaviors that could harm them.

To get out of this pattern, the Fourth Born needs to perceive him or herself as a grown-up among grown-ups rather than as a child with older siblings. This new perception can produce a gentler, kinder Fourth Born.

The above does not apply to all Fourth Borns. Many are kind, gentle, and caring human beings to start with. They grew without having to fight their way through older siblings. Or, perhaps they learned to be gentle anyway by seeing themselves as adults.

BIRTH ORDER DEPRESSION

ALBERT EINSTEIN SAID "Everything should be made as simple as possible, but not simpler." That dictum has been ignored by those dealing with Birth Order. When Birth Order is made too simple as in oldest, middle and youngest child, it becomes useless by dealing in generalities rather than specifics in personality. May I suggest how Birth Order can be made a little less simple so that it is much more effective in understanding personality? How about five Birth Order personalities – Only, First, Second, Third and Fourth Born with repeat cycles in large families? It is more complex but still as simple as possible.

In order to grasp the five personalities of Birth Order we can look at how they each experience depression. This will allow us to see how Birth Order personality develops, some of the basic issues of each Birth Order, and how psychotherapy can be used with each Birth Order.

Birth Order is developed very early, usually by age two. Each Birth Order has negative experiences that generate an unacceptable feeling that has to be hidden from others. In the process of hiding the feeling from others, the feeling also gets hidden from self. That hidden feeling becomes a strong influence throughout life and is the source of Birth Order depression. The hidden feelings are fear, sadness, shame, stupidity, and loneliness.

Parents are eager to introduce the Only Child to new experiences that may feel scary to the child. They may urge the child to take first steps before she's ready, compel her to pet the goat at the petting zoo, or perform before the family. When she shows reluctance, her parents tell her to not be afraid. That does not stop her from being afraid but thinking that fear is unacceptable she has to hide it. Life becomes boring as she avoids doing things that make her uncomfortable, fails to find things exciting, and looks for people who will give her the excitement she cannot find for herself. The active ingredient in excitement is fear that gives zest to life. Without it, the Only can become depressed.

To relieve the depression the focus needs to change from hiding fear to enjoying excitement. Phrased in language that speaks to the subconscious, the therapy is "Never get so interested in hiding your fear that you forget to enjoy excitement." The subconscious responds by changing the focus so that the Only goes from being a spectator to participant, from fixing others to accepting them. Doing things and accepting people become a source of excitement and depression lifts.

Parents often expect a lot of the First Born. When the new baby comes the First Born is expected to understand that baby needs care and he must share mother's love. He's too young to understand and is used to getting mother's love on demand. Now he sits on the couch watching mother having too much fun with the baby and giving baby the love he used to get. The loss makes him sad but he cannot express the sadness because he has to understand. So, he hides the sadness even from himself so that it becomes a source of depression. The depression often keeps him from expressing his opinion, from telling others what he wants, and makes him acquire things that do not satisfy.

The First Born needs to change the focus from sadness to happiness. The therapy that does it says "Never get so interested in hiding your sadness that you forget to enjoy being happy." The effect is that the First Born goes from being gloomy to being happy, from impressing others to respecting them. He no longer has to live with inner sadness though he can get sad over a genuine loss better than before and he no longer has to work hard to get love from others in order to get over being sad.

The second child gets her personality by what the First Born does. One day, the second child discovers she can produce colors with crayons on a page from the coloring book. She is thrilled by the result. She has produced random colorful lines on the page that she can hardly wait so show mother. The First Born has also colored a page from the coloring book but it is a picture, not just lines. Of course, the First Born gets to mother first and she admires his picture. When she sees what the Second Born has done she assures her that she will eventually do as well. The thrill the Second Born felt becomes shame as she compares their results. However, the shame has to be hidden because she has to think that she will do better in the future. That hidden shame drives the Second Born to strive toward perfection, criticize what others do and to not accept compliments. Not being able to find satisfaction in what she does the hidden shame turns into depression.

Depression therapy for the Second Born shifts her focus from shame to success. Her subconscious makes the shift when she is told, "Never get so interested in hiding your shame that you forget to enjoy success." The effect on the Second Born is to go from pessimism to optimism, from criticizing others to affirming them. Becoming able to celebrate her success she becomes a happier person having a more positive effect on all those around her.

The Third Born becomes Third Born in reaction to the Second Born attempting to pass the hidden feeling of shame to him. When the Third Born is creating a structure from Legos, the Second Born pushes him aside, makes a better structure, and ridicules the way he was going about it so that he feels stupid. However, he does not want to allow her to think she got to him so he hides the feeling of stupidity from her and from himself. The hidden feeling of stupidity sometimes drives the Third Born to take dangerous risks to prove how capable he is, to choose friends that make him look good in comparison, and to think for others so they can feel stupid instead. Because these strategies do not overcome the hidden feeling of stupidity the Third Born becomes depressed.

The cure for the Third Born is to change the focus from the hidden feeling of stupidity to freedom to thinking. This is done by telling him, "Never get so interested in hiding your stupidity that you forget to enjoy thinking." As he shifts focus, he becomes more sensible about risks he takes, more open to what others think, and more open to people who do better than he does. He discovers that he can come up ideas that others like. The depression lifts.

With three older siblings, the Fourth Born experiences lots of injustice with the biggest injustice being left out of their play. The only hope for the Fourth Born is to have Mom make the older children include him but even if it works, the older siblings find ways to punish her for appealing to mother so that playing with them is no fun anyway. To get along, the Fourth Born has to hide her loneliness from self and others. This becomes a form of depression that gives Fourth Borns anger for no apparent reason, a tendency to strain relationships by being unfair to others, and causes them to feel isolated. It can become frustrating for others to try to relate to the depressed Fourth Born.

For the Fourth Born to recover from this depression, she must move from a focus on the hidden feeling of loneliness to fairness. This shift is made in response to the statement, "Never get so interested in hiding your loneliness that you forget to enjoy being fair." This produces the effect of going from being a loner to joining, from controlling others to cooperating with them. The Fourth Born gains the ability to interact with others, to feel comfortable in a group, and to have a positive attitude in place of anger. The depression is lifted.

There is more to Birth Order but to obey Einstein's words I'm keeping this as simple as possible. There is much more to learn.

BIRTH ORDER DEPRESSION

INTERVENTION

HERE ARE SOME things that you can say to intervene upon depression.

Only – Never get so interested in hiding your fears that you forget to enjoy life.
Moves the Only from spectator to participant.

First – Never get so interested in hiding your sadness that you forget to enjoy love.
Moves the First from impressing to respecting.

Second – Never get so interested in hiding your pain that you forget to enjoy success.
Moves the Second from pessimism to optimism.

Third – Never get so interested in hiding your anger that you forget to enjoy caring.
Moves the Third from rescuing to helping.

Fourth – Never get so interested in hiding your loneliness that you forget to enjoy relationships.
Moves the Fourth from being a loner to joining.

SITUATIONAL DEPRESSION

Note: Check with your doctor before changing or stopping any medication.

DEPRESSION IS A limiting emotional state often experienced as a "bad" feeling. If it is caused by a situation, it passes when the situation changes. If it is caused by memories, it exists without reference to your situation. In this chapter, we'll look at depression arising from your circumstances.

Each Birth Order experiences depression differently. The Only Child experiences frustration, the First Born is oppressed by guilt, the Second Born gets testy, the Third Born pursues ways to feel good often resulting in addictions, and the Fourth Born feels anger toward self and others. The roots of situational depression are the same for every Birth Order.

Originally, everyone learned to get things done by feeling bad. In the crib, we cried when we were hungry, uncomfortable in our diaper, or wanting attention. These experiences planted memories of success by feeling bad. When we face a difficult situation it is as if our subconscious says "I know what to do! If I feel bad enough long enough that will take care of it." Of course, it no longer works. But, it keeps us from thinking of other strategies because subconsciously we are committed to getting things done by feeling bad.

As we got older, other strategies replaced feeling

bad. Parents and others would tell us to stop crying, whining, or pouting in order to get what we wanted. We understood that we were to feel okay rather than using bad feelings. We had to learn other ways of getting things done.

We experience these memories when faced with a bad circumstance. We struggle to feel okay without success. Our memories tell us that we have to feel okay but we cannot feel okay. This inner struggle creates the emotional state of situational depression.

To relieve this depression we need to have your subconscious disconnect from those memories that make you feel okay. Those memories, rather than enabling you to feel okay, activate the memories of getting things done by feeling bad. To change that, tell yourself (your subconscious) to

"Forget the memories that make you feel okay."

On the other hand, at times you have been able to feel okay when things were bad. We want those memories to support your behavior now, so we activate them. Tell yourself,

"Remember the memories that let you feel okay."

Your circumstances may not change but your reaction to them will. You'll be able to think more effectively than you could before. It will take a day or two to notice the effect.

Remember: Check with your doctor before changing or stopping any medication.

EARLY MEMORIES CREATE BIRTH ORDER

THE ACTUAL MEMORIES that create Birth Order personalities go back to such an early age that they surface as feelings only. A person does not consciously remember what he/she saw or heard at that age, just the feelings. These feelings drive Birth Order behavior without appearing as memories. Thus Birth Order personality comes into being by age two. The exceptions are the First Born who can become First Born when the second child is born, any time up to age five. The Only Child is an Only from birth.

THE TRUE PERFECTIONIST

THE WORD "PERFECTIONIST" probably makes you think of the person who has everything in order. The home is organized, time is scheduled, post-it reminders keep this person on track. Everything looks good. This person may look like a perfectionist but is not. This person just wants to do things right.

The true perfectionist is one who pays attention to every detail. This kind of behavior is not possible in all things so the perfectionist chooses limited areas for perfection. The true perfectionist is the Second Born. The Second Born teen-age girl may spend hours primping in the bathroom but lets her room be a mess. The Second Born carpenter strives for perfection making cabinets but lets his truck be a mess. The Second Born accountant may keep perfect books for an employer while neglecting his or her own finances. The perfectionism of the Second Born is driven by feelings of inadequacy arising from having to compete with an older First Born sibling. During childhood the First Born outdid the Second Born to get mother's attention, leaving the Second Born feeling inadequate.

Who is the person who wants to do things right? That's the Only Child. Quite often the oldest child is an Only Child despite having younger siblings. Many birth order researchers mistakenly attribute Only Child characteristics to the First Born.

THE PERILS OF BEING STRONG

ONE BIRTH ORDER personality is compelled to be strong, emotionally strong. This is the Third Born. In early childhood, this one got teased mercilessly by the older Second Born. After appealing to mother many times, the Third Born gave up, deciding to not let it bother them. Perhaps mother suggested this attitude by saying "Just ignore him." The Third Born motto became "No problem, it doesn't bother me any."

The Third Born became fearless. The most fearless are those with an older Second Born sibling of the same sex. These are the people who take risks just to prove they are fearless. They are the military heroes who fearlessly overcome an enemy position single handedly. The teasing would not be as great from a Second Born of the opposite sex - in fact it might have been welcome attention as the child got older. So the Third Born with a Second Born sibling of the opposite sex tends to be a cautious type Third Born.

In being fearless, these Third Borns have to shut off any feelings of weakness, desires, wanting, fear, or anything else that could portray weakness. Since they shut off such feelings, they are unable to care for themselves emotionally. They just take care of others. Sometimes the inner emotional need becomes so great it drives the Third Born to extreme behavior - like reckless spending, drinking binges, or risky behavior. This swing between extremes may be the basis for bipolar disorder.

THE HIDDEN PERSONALITY

THERE IS A personality no one understands, including professionals who are supposed to understand people. This personality does not show up on psychological tests, is unknown to counselors, and is not described in personality profiles. How can this be? Birth Order has the answer.

In a family, the oldest child does not have to understand the next child, or in fact any of the other children. The First Born can overpower the others so there is no need to understand them. The Second Born has to understand the First Born in order to deal with this sibling who has so much power. The Second Born, however, does not have to understand the Third or Fourth Born because the Second Born can overpower them. The Fourth Born has to understand the older siblings to deal with them but no one understands the Fourth Born. This carries into adult life.

The Fourth Born hides emotionally, mentally, and sometimes physically in order to live with being misunderstood. The Fourth Born early on gives up on anyone understanding. So, there is no input from Fourth Borns to enable others to understand them even in adult life. Since they are in a small minority it is not obvious that they are not being understood. If people experience a Fourth Born in their lives they settle for thinking that this person is strange, unreasonable, and just different from the rest of us.

AGE DIFFERENCES IN BIRTH ORDER

A LARGE AGE gap can affect Birth Order. If there are more than five years between the first and second child, they will be Only Children in personality. The second child can become a First Born if there is another child born within five years.

If there is a gap of at least five years between all the siblings they are all Onlies. However, a pseudo birth order pattern develops. With Only Children, the second one does not want to be like the first so the second one appears very different from the first one. A third child would appear quite different from the first two. What looks like Birth Order personalities is actually superficial differences. Underneath they all have the same personality.

Once there are a First and Second Born there can be up to 14 years between the second and third to still get a Third Born. There can be up to 10 years between third and fourth child to still develop a Fourth Born personality in the fourth born.

BIRTH ORDER MATE CHOICES

BIRTH ORDER INFLUENCES whom you are likely to marry. The greatest influence is from the parent of the same sex. As a child growing up, you have companionship, whether it is good or bad, with the parent of the same sex. Since every love relationship starts out as companionship, that relationship influences your choice.

If you are an Only Child you find yourself attracted to the same Birth Order as your parent. First through Fourth Borns are attracted to the next Birth Order following the parent. The companionship as a child has you learning to interact from the same personality if an Only or from the next Birth Order if you are First Through Fourth. An Only Child parent would make you drawn to an Only.

If the parent is a Fourth Born the child would be drawn to an Only if First through Fourth. The Only Child of a Fourth Born would be drawn to a Fourth Born.

Other factors also influence choice of partner. There is a natural attraction between an Only and a Second Born who often experience love at first sight. It tends to be a good relationship. A First Born and a Third Born who follows a Second Born sibling of the opposite sex tend to be drawn to each other. Two First Borns never marry. If both are the oldest in the family, one or both will be something other than First Born.

A poor relationship with the parent of the same sex forecasts a poor marital relationship. Marrying someone of the "wrong" Birth Order can cause stress. Both of these cases require higher maintenance than other marriages. However, they can be happy relationships.

Regular use of alcohol or drugs can destroy an otherwise good relationship. These substances disrupt the nonverbal communication that is so important for a good relationship.

PREDICTING DOMESTIC ABUSE

MOST PEOPLE WHO marry an abusive person have no hint that abuse will happen. Many a woman has spent her wedding night in tears because the man she got was nothing like the man she thought she married. They plaintively ask why they could not tell he would abuse. They often stay in the marriage with the hope that the man they knew before marriage will return to make the marriage happy.

Men marry abusive women almost as frequently as women marry abusive men. The dynamic is the same - they are blindsided because they never expected the abuse. They live with the hope that the person they knew before is gone temporarily, soon to return.

Is there an indicator that a person is likely to be abusive? Yes, there is but it is the opposite of what you think the indicator might be. You might think that there would be red flags of abusive behavior ahead of time. Sometimes there are but often there are no obvious red flags. Before marriage, most of the time, the man or woman who is going to be abusive is one of the nicest people you could meet.

Here's the signal for future abuse. The person who is going to be abusive puts you on a pedestal before marriage. He (or she) tells you how wonderful you are, how he enjoys everything about you, how great your marriage will be, how he likes your personality, and how you are the greatest thing that has ever happened to him. He is so happy to have you in his life, to be able to contemplate

162

coming home to you after a hard day"s work, and to enjoy cuddling up with you. You feel like a princess on the throne. Here is a man who adores you without question. Why would you think he could be abusive?

As this man is telling you how wonderful you are, he is also telling you what he expects after you are married. You are the person who is going to make him happy and you better make him happy or else. When it turns out that you are human after all instead of a princess, he is furious. He told you how wonderful you are and you took it all in. You did not tell him you were human instead of wonderful so now his rage is "justified" toward you because you deceived him. You are not doing what you are supposed to do, make him feel great. Of course you cannot because you are human, not a magician.

Of all the Birth Orders, the most likely to be abusive is the Fourth Born. The Fourth grew up in powerlessness at the mercy of older siblings. Feeling helpless, this person resolved that when he grew up he would have someone in his life that would make him happy. When he found you and told you how wonderful you are and you did not disagree, he got very excited. He had found the person who would magically make him happy, even ecstatic. When you did not do that immediately after the wedding, he was devastated. Extremely disappointed, he decided you lied to him and that he had every right to be angry at you.

A person of another Birth Order could be abusive also. The clues are the same. You are made to be a princess on a pedestal from which you will grant his wish to be happy. The alternative healthy start is with both accepting each other as human beings with no unrealistic expectations. Your red warning flag is when he or she insists you are wonderfully more than human.

The pleasure the abuser feels before marriage is actually in anticipation of what is to come. The future abuser reasons that whatever pleasure comes from relating now will be even greater after marriage. His expectations soar with every moment of pleasure he has with you during courtship. Imagine the letdown when the anticipated magic does not occur after the wedding. No wonder he is so angry!

SOME BIRTH ORDER

OCCUPATIONS

THERE ARE SOME occupations that are Birth Order specific. For example, novelists are mostly Second Born. Suppressing their feelings, Second Borns find it easy to express their feelings in print. Also, artists, both visual and auditory, are often Second Borns. Accountants are usually Second Borns although you can find some Onlies among them. A Second Born who comes up through the ranks of accounting, where they do very well, to the rank of CEO often do very poorly in that position. The very things that made them good at accounting - paying attention to detail - makes them poor at running a company.

Radio disk jockeys are typically Only Children. It is the Only who can imagine an audience, relate to them comfortably, and entertain a real audience. Onlies as organizers often make good CEOs. They are also found in the ranks of teachers.

Researching fits First Borns. Their research type thinking makes them comfortable figuring things out. They have an interest in studying relationships because it is an area of weakness for them. As the oldest in the family, they did not have to learn how to relate as children since they could overpower siblings.

Selling is an excellent field for Third Borns, although some Third Borns would never consider it. The Third Born's desire to help people motivates them in selling so they need a product they believe actually helps people. Give them such a product, the faith that they are helping people, and let them go. They'll do wonders in selling. This is all the motivation any salesperson needs, so trying to motivate sales people with money tends to draw the wrong kind of person into selling. However, making a top salesperson into the sales manager is a mistake often made. The motivation of helping people that makes a good salesperson gets in the way of challenging a sales force.

The philosophers are Fourth Borns. Given their propensity to analyze endlessly they can philosophize well. The best singers are often Fourth Borns. This seems to be because of early experiences in which people did not listen to them except when they were singing. With this incentive, they developed the ability to sing to compensate for not getting a hearing.

THINKING PATTERNS

EACH BIRTH ORDER personality has it's own thinking pattern.

The Only Child is the organizer. This is the person who wants everything in order, a schedule worked out, and questions answered. This person walks into a familiar room and notices immediately if something has been moved. This person thinks a lot about time and finds it easy to say he does not have time. "Time management" is an Only Child concept because you cannot "manage" time, you can only manage activities. The Only imagines you can manage time.

The pattern of thinking for the First Born is research. The First Born does not know what to think until he or she finds out what someone else thinks. Once the First Born knows what someone else thinks, then he or she knows what to think. This fits well with research where you find out what others think.

The pattern of thinking for the Second Born is evaluation. A perfectionist, the Second Born studies details looking for flaws in order to evaluate something that is not perfect. The first response by a Second Born to a new concept, idea, or thought is to question what might be wrong with it.

The pattern of thinking for the Third Born is comparison thinking, sometimes called lateral thinking. When the Third Born encounters something, he or she immediately compares it to something else. Often, the comparison generates a new discovery. It is the mind of the inventor such as Thomas Edison who was the youngest of seven brothers (since Birth Order repeats the seventh child is a Third Born.)

The pattern of thinking for the Fourth Born is analysis. To avoid being trapped, the Fourth Born looks at things from every angle, above, below, inside, outside, forward, back, and repeats it again. Thinking on a subject can take not just hours but days. Conclusions are never final because further analysis might revise the conclusion. Sometimes unwarranted conclusions can be drawn by over analyzing a trivial bit of information.

JUSTICE

EACH BIRTH ORDER has its own sense of justice. That means there are five types of justice.

The Only Child believes in equal justice. Everyone should get an equal piece of the pie. If one gets more than another, that's unfair. Giving gifts at holiday time, an Only Child mother may feel compelled to give each child gifts of the same monetary value. One mother went so far as to tape coins on gifts to make them all equal in value. This sense of justice comes from organizational thinking.

First Borns believe in just desserts because love to them is conditional. They live in a world without love so love has to be earned. People should get what they deserve. If they have done well, they should be rewarded accordingly. If they deserve punishment, that's what they should get.

Onlies and Firsts believe there can be justice in the world. The other three Birth Orders believe that life is unfair.

Since life is unfair, the Second Born thinks you must do what is necessary. You don't expect to be fair with other people because life is unfair. You just do what you have to do without apology. This comes from the Second Born inclination toward suppressing feelings to operate from evaluative thinking. For example, the Second Born employer may lay off employees without any feeling because it is "necessary."

The Third Born has a more compassionate point of

view. Since life is unfair, you must do what you can to help victims of injustice. The Third Born promotes a Robin Hood type of response to injustice by taking from those who have it to give to those who need it. This person may believe this is the function of government. On a personal level, the Third Born may in fact be unfair to one person in order to help someone else.

The Fourth Born has a sense of justice borne out of a feeling of helplessness. When helpless, you cannot do what is necessary or take from those who have it to give to those who don't or do anything about the injustice you suffer. So, when you suffer injustice all you can do is retaliate, i.e., get even. The Biblical injunction of an eye for an eye and a tooth for a tooth is a concept that originated from Fourth Borns in antiquity, not widely accepted by the other Birth Orders, thank goodness! Sometimes Fourth Borns destroy their own lives in the process of getting even with someone else. For example, witness shootings in the workplace where the shooter ends up killing himself.

LONG TERM EFFECT OF BIRTH ORDER

WHAT WILL THE long-term effect be of understanding Birth Order? One First Born (they are future oriented) asked, "As this information becomes more common in our society, will not the next generation sort of grow beyond it?" I think the answer is yes. We can't tell till we get there. We do know that observation changes behavior. Once Birth Order is generally understood or at least accepted we can be confident it will change behavior in general. We are a long way from that general acceptance.

Observation changes behavior because it causes a person to dissociate from it. If you tell someone who is angry "You sound like you're angry" or "You look like you're angry" the person will stop being angry in few moments because the person has dissociated from the anger. It works with anxiety as well if you tell the person "You look scared." It does not work to tell a person "Don't be angry" or "Don't be scared" because it leaves them associated with the feeling. In fact, the subconscious drops the "don't" so that instead of "Don't be scared" the subconscious hears "Be scared." If you want to scare someone just tell the person "Don't be scared!"

Birth Order is useful for individuals because it allows them to look at their own behavior. This dissociated view enables change. With Birth Order understanding, a person gets beyond being defensive to look at his or her own behavior.

171

BIRTH ORDER T-SHIRTS

THE ESSENCE OF Birth Order personalities can be expressed as T-shirt sayings on the front and the back.

The Only Child T-shirt says, "Leave Me Alone" on the front with "I'd rather do it myself" on the back. This reflects the Only Child tendency to live in his or her own world.

The First Born T-shirt says on the front, "I don't know" and on the back "What do you think?" This reflects the First Born being out of touch with self so that he or she needs to know what someone else thinks. The words "I don't know" are common in First Born conversation.

The Second Born T-shirt says on the front, "That won't work" and on the back "It's not good enough." This reflects the Second Born evaluative thinking.

The Third Born T-shirt says on the front, "No problem" and on the back "It doesn't bother me any." Third Borns often use the words "No problem" in conversation, especially as a response to a thank you rather than saying "You're welcome." These words reflect the Third Born needing to appear strong so nothing is a problem.

The Fourth Born T-shirt says on the front, "Life isn't easy" and on the back "You have to try hard." This reflects the Fourth Born seeking to feel grown up by doing difficult things.

A WALK IN THE WOODS

BIRTH ORDER BEHAVIORS can be characterized by a walk in the woods. An Only Child taking a walk in the woods sticks to the path, reads the signs along the way, and starts back when necessary to get back at the right time. The Only stays organized on the walk.

A First Born picks a distant goal, walks through the difficult part of the woods, trips over roots, falls into the creek, gets all dirty, and is unable to reach the goal. However, if he were to reach the goal, he would be disappointed. Goals have to be high enough to never be completely attainable.

A Second Born walks around in circles in the woods, watching her feet, discovering interesting pieces of wood along the way. She may bump her head into low lying branches as she watches her feet.

A Third Born goes into the woods only if someone else wants to go and needs help. The Third Born takes this person through the most difficult part of the woods insisting that the person be strong. The Third Born does not go into the woods for his or her own sake.

The Fourth Born does not go into the woods at all. He stands outside the woods, tells others where to go and how to get there. That's why so many coaches are Fourth Born.

BIRTH ORDER EYE MOVEMENTS

ONE CLUE TO personality is how people move their eyes. This involuntary movement can help identify Birth Order in social settings where other indications are hidden.

An Only Child has a rapid eye movement that takes in everything in their environment. In a room they notice the pictures, furniture, decorations, knick-knacks, and arrangements. The mental process of organizing drives this eye movement.

A First Born looks at people, especially faces. The First Born does not look at environment. So the First Born does not see the environment but watches people. The subconscious need for attention drives this eye movement.

A Second Born will focus on something in the environment, engaging it in a steady gaze. The need for perfection drives this fixed type of eye movement. Perfection is only possible if you limit the scope of what you observe.

A Third Born has an eye movement similar to that of the Only except it is slower. The Third Born scans the environment rather slowly, often going back to what he or she has already viewed. The Third Born mental process of comparing drives this eye movement.

A Fourth Born tends to look forward at nothing in particular. Once in a while the Fourth Born will look to one side or the other without turning the head as if trying to see if someone is sneaking up on him or her, something that may have happened frequently when older siblings did it to startle the Fourth Born.

These eye movements are best observed when persons are in an unfamiliar environment. You are not apt to see these movements at home but rather at social events, shopping malls, amusement parks, or other places where people gather.

These eye movements are a natural interaction with an unfamiliar environment. Lack of these eye movements suggests the person has an agenda that does not include interacting with the environment. Lack of normal eye movements might be a way of identifying terrorists before they strike.

MIDDLE CHILD

IN 1918, WHEN psychiatrist Alfred Adler first suggested Birth Order, he defined it as being oldest, middle, and youngest child. He was a middle child himself so had a special feeling for that position. In fact, he thought first borns were arrogant and youngest born were spoiled so that left the middle child who was okay.

Ever since then, researchers have tried to figure out the middle child. It turns out that there is no middle child personality. The middle child can be any of five Birth Order personalities.

The middle child can be an Only when there are five year spans between each of the children. The middle child can be a First Born if the oldest remains an Only and other children follow. The middle child can be a Second Born, the most common middle child. The middle child can be a Third Born if there are four or more children or a Fourth Born if there are five or more children. Alfred Adler taught that regardless of how many children there were, there was one first born, one last born and all the children in between were middle children.

Each child has a Birth Order personality. Middle child is not one of these personalities.

BABY OF THE FAMILY

PEOPLE OFTEN THINK of the youngest child in the family as the baby as if that were a particular Birth Order personality. It is not.

The youngest in the family can be of any Birth Order except a First Born. To have a First Born requires a Second Born so the youngest child cannot be a First Born.

The youngest child can be a Second, Third or Fourth Born if that is the number of children in the family. The youngest child can be an Only if this child is the fifth child. Age difference with the Fourth Born does not matter.

Because of exceptions, the youngest child may not have the personality dictated by the numbers. It is always best to determine personality by characteristics rather than rely on the numbers. The numbers are just a beginning indicator.

BENEFIT OF KNOWING BIRTH ORDER

THE BEST REASON for studying your Birth Order is to enable you to overcome it. Birth Order is a set of coping strategies developed at home in childhood. These strategies enabled you to cope with your siblings (or lack of them), your parents, and with the family situation. When you got old enough, you were able to learn to cope with the world through interaction with your peers. If you did not have a good experience with peers, you may try to cope with the world through your Birth Order strategies.

Your Birth Order behavior is not apparent to you until someone describes it. Once you know it, you can begin to get beyond it. Knowing yourself is like seeing your face. You have to look in a mirror. The mirror for your personality is your peer group.

Even if you function well in the world, your Birth Order comes out at home. Your spouse and children experience your Birth Order as no one else does. You are literally a different person at home than you are away from home. Knowing your Birth Order has the greatest benefit on what happens at home.

BIRTH ORDER IN BUSINESS

A BUSINESS IS most likely to prosper if the right Birth Order personalities hold the right positions.

The CEO is best if an Only. The Only sees the overall picture, pays attention to organization, wants to get things done right, and creates a good emotional climate. This CEO can stand alone in a way the other Birth Orders cannot.

The First Born is best in research and development. Given the research thinking pattern of the First Born, this person is open to new ideas and can accept them from outsiders as well as from employees. The First Born does not think up ideas in isolation so development is practical.

The accounting department calls for a Second Born. The Second Born's interest in details, perfectionism, and self-discipline equip this person for number crunching. In accounting, perfection is not only desirable but necessary, thus fitting the Second Born's penchant for perfection.

The super salesperson for the company will be a Third Born. He or she wants to help people with a good product, providing the incentive to sell. The Third Born moves from customer to customer without being derailed by rejection. One successful deal motivates the Third Born on to the next deal without stopping to celebrate the last triumph.

The Fourth Born fits the role of sales manager. The Fourth Born is a natural people manager from having studied his or her older siblings all those years of growing up. Also, the Fourth Born subconsciously expects others to be Third Born like his older sibling who made him into a Fourth Born. The Fourth Born recognizes qualities that make the Third Born a Third Born so this sales manager builds on the natural strengths of the Third Born salesperson.

Companies make two major mistakes in promoting people. One is promoting the head of accounting to the position of CEO. This is often done when a company is looking to be conservative after having done well. To save money, the Second Born CEO cuts back on employee benefits, squeezes more production out of fewer employees, eliminates overtime, and keeps wages low. Employees become demoralized so that they no longer enthusiastically support the company. Production becomes shabby, customer relations suffer, and employees fail to warn about potential pitfalls. Without employee loyalty, a company suffers.

The second major mistake is promoting the best salesperson to the position of sales manager under the theory that the good salesperson can clone himself. In promoting the super salesperson to sales manager, the company loses a good salesperson to gain a poor sales manager. The qualities that make for good selling do not make for good managing. The Third Born sales manager fails to challenge the sales force as he or she is selling them on the idea of selling.

There are exceptions. For example, a Second Born who becomes CEO of a company already in deep difficulty is often able to bring the company to good health. The attention to detail is probably the contributing factor. A Third Born who starts his or her own company, can function well as CEO because of the compassion the Third Born has for employees. This would not work in an existing company because the Third Born management style that really trusts people, can be scary to the board.

BIRTH ORDER LEARNING STYLES

AN ONLY LEARNS by getting organized. This is the student who is most likely to ask questions about logistics - why, how, what, and where. He or she wants to get the information necessary to get organized. In studying, the Only gets things organized. Sometimes getting organized cuts into the time needed for study. The Only is apt to find studying difficult unless he or she allows a transition time of 20 to 30 minutes between attending classes and sitting down to study.

The First Born learns best when he or she understands the purpose of what is being studied. This relates to the First Born's goal orientation that imagines the future. The present needs to contribute to this imagination for the First Born to be motivated. When daydreaming about the future gets in the way, the First Born needs to focus on each small task as it is completed allowing a feeling of satisfaction. It is the little things that add up to big things.

The Second Born pays attention to details. This is the student who is most apt to find errors in the textbook, tests, and in what the instructor says. The Second Born is usually best able to focus on the task at hand with the self-discipline to get the job done. The Second Born can pass up the opportunity to party to get homework done. Facing a deadline, the Second Born may either get a project done well in advance or may wait till the last minute to pull an all-nighter to get it done. For a satisfying educational experience, the Second Born needs to include activities done just for the emotion involved.

The Third Born tends to be laid back. Easily distracted, the Third Born may spend too much time socializing, pursing interesting activities, and helping others. The Third Born is the one who gets creative ideas related to the subject being studied. Some of these ideas are very good while others are off the wall. The Third Born who allows caring for self, may do better at education that is for his or her benefit.

The Fourth Born may get hung up on analyzing everything. Analyzing may take so much time that the Fourth Born is unable to keep up, get everything done, and gets to feeling overwhelmed. The Fourth Born is unable to reach conclusions based on learning. Since Fourth Borns' isolation feeds the analyzing, associating with others can help. Listening to others lets the Fourth Born determine what is important.

WHEN THE OLDEST IS INDEPENDENT

ABOUT ONE-THIRD OF the time, the oldest child in a family is an Only psychologically. This frequently happens even with a small age gap with the next child. The oldest child starts out as an Only until the next child is born. At that time, the Only becomes a First Born unless someone, like grandma, is there to make sure the oldest child does not lose love because baby is there. In two or three days, the oldest child is used to the baby so is in no danger of becoming a First Born

If the oldest child in the family is an independent sort of person, this is likely what has happened. The oldest is an Only with the next child being a First Born if there is at least another child. This throws the numbers off all down the line. The third child will be a Second Born, the fourth child a Third Born, and the fifth child will be a Fourth Born.

It's always best to check Birth Order characteristics to verify the Birth Order personality. Numbers are not enough.

LOVE AT FIRST SIGHT

ONE BIRTH ORDER combination can experience love at first sight when they meet. Of the twenty-five possible Birth Order pairings, this is the only couple likely to fall in love with their first encounter.

This lucky couple is a Second Born and an Only Child. The Only Child is drawn to the Second as he or she senses the Second Born's reliability that permits the Only to be organized. The Second Born feels the attraction for the Only as he or she picks up on the Only Child's propensity to do things right which fits so well with the Second Born perfectionism. These qualities are conveyed non-verbally so they are not aware of why they are attracted to each other. All they know is that they have a strong attraction to each other very quickly. This usually presages a good marriage.

No other couple seems to experience this kind of immediate connection. They may find an attraction to each other from the start but without the intensity of the Only/Second couple.

LISTENING STYLES

EACH OF THE Birth Orders listens for certain things. Only Children listen for things they can talk about in their experience. First Borns listen to agree or disagree. Second Borns listen for details. Third Borns listen for ideas. Fourth Borns tend to not listen.

Of course, at times everyone also listens to understand, to gain information, to relate, and to learn. When you have a problem listening, check to see if you are listening according to your Birth Order personality instead of really listening. When another person does not seem to listen, that person's Birth Order may tell you what the person is really listening for. It's easier to deal with things when you know what is going on.

AGING WITH BIRTH ORDER

SOMETIMES BIRTH ORDER stays strong throughout life. But for many people, apparent Birth Order Effects diminish as they get older, being the least apparent when they are in their fifties. Usually the stresses of raising a family, coping with advancing a career, and marital friction become less during the fifties. After a person reaches retirement age, Birth Order characteristics tend to return. The limitations of age, stress of illness, and the inability to leave home tend to bring back the effects of Birth Order.

Understanding one's own Birth Order improves life at any age. Understanding others' Birth Orders improves relationships at any age. And, understanding Birth Order is one way to prepare for the retirement years.

WHEN MOTHER CAUSES BIRTH ORDER

A MOTHER UNDER stress when her oldest child is around two years of age can create a Birth Order personality in her child that is not First Born. This means the oldest child can be Second, Third, or Fourth because of the mother's interaction with the child.

The Birth Order created in the child depends not only on Mother's Birth Order but also on the sex of the child. If the child is a boy, he takes on the same Birth Order as Mother's. If the child is a girl, she takes on the next Birth Order following Mother's.

With a Second Born mother, the daughter becomes Third Born in personality. With a Third Born mother, the daughter takes on the Fourth Born personality. The effect does not seem to happen with a First Born mother. Remember that for this to happen, the mother has to be stressed out by a bad marriage, dire financial circumstances, or an extreme situation.

The Second Born mother under stress produces Second Born in her son, a Third Born mom produces Third Born, and a Fourth Born mom produces Fourth Born in her son.

The rest of the children will follow in order. For example, if the oldest is a Third Born, the next child will be a Fourth Born.

HOW GENDER AFFECTS BIRTH ORDER

GENDER AFFECTS HOW Birth Order is expressed but it does not determine Birth Order personality. In fact, it is the difference in genders between siblings that determines how Birth Order is expressed. A Second Born with an older sibling of the opposite sex is more mellow than one with the same sex older sibling. A Third Born with an opposite sex older sibling tends to be more cautious than a Third Born who has a same sex older sibling. A Fourth Born tends not to be rough if the older siblings are of the opposite sex. A First Born with an opposite sex younger sibling tends to be more self-confident than the First Born with a same sex younger sibling. An Only has no siblings but the female Only will probably express emotions more easily than the male Only.

Women tend to be more relationship oriented than men who tend to be goal oriented. At the midlife transition between ages 38 and 42 they change roles so that women get more goal oriented and men become more relationship oriented. Look at eighty-year old people - the men are in the coffee shop visiting with each other while grandma is busy making afghans for her grandchildren.

STUDENT ACHIEVEMENT

HERE ARE SOME observations about student achievement by Birth Order. On the average, Only children will achieve higher because of their desire to do things right and because of their organizational thinking. Only Children students tend to have difficulty with algebra because they try to organize it rather than doing it step by step. They get frustrated when they are not able to see the outcome at the beginning.

First Borns do well in order to impress others. They tend to do best when they have instructors who give them praise. In fact, they will tend to look for feedback by asking questions that do not need to be asked, checking with the teacher to see if they are doing something right, and paying close attention to how other children do their projects, not to copy them but to surpass them. They like to work with groups where they can hear others' ideas. Their area of interest is research especially in the area of human behavior.

Second Borns do well when study involves details. They tend to do better in math, art, and music but may not do as well in social sciences which involve understanding emotion. They tend to write well, do neat work, and turn homework in on time. Because of their evaluative thinking, they're the first to notice when teacher makes a mistake.

Third Borns do well if allowed to express their creativity. They generate lots of ideas, becoming motivated when they feel their ideas are respected. Put under pressure, they tend to rebel, not wanting to do what they're told. They do well in problem solving. They also like to help other students, often associating with the poor achievers.

Fourth Borns are analytical. They tend to do well in social sciences and philosophy. They like to be challenged and tend to rise to challenges. In the classroom, they tend to be either passive or aggressive. Because of their analytical thinking they do well when they are complimented on their thinking. They tend to see through teachers' efforts to influence them and are thus able to manipulate teachers.

The above descriptions can verify a student's Birth Order. Their behavior in the classroom may confirm their Birth Order personality. Or, their behavior may indicate that their Birth Order personality is something other than place in the family would dictate.

BIRTH ORDER SITUATIONS

BIRTH ORDER DEVELOPS in one of five situations experienced by a child. A child may be alone, lose love to a younger sibling, competes with an older sibling showing off to get attention, be stifled by an older sibling who ridicules his or her ideas, or be made to feel immature by an older sibling. When ignored by an older sibling, the child experiences being alone.

Birth Order is developed under the intensity of emotion that is only experienced in the home. Lacking the intensity of emotion... daycare, school, playground, or other experiences do not develop Birth Order. They enable the child to develop social skills but Birth Order is developed at home.

A child who is alone or ignored by the next older sibling who is Fourth Born becomes an Only Child personality. An oldest child who loses mother's attention to the new baby becomes First Born. The second child who must compete with the oldest child becomes Second Born. The third child has to endure but does not have to compete with the Second Born who is more interested in perfection than showing off so becomes Third Born. The fourth child does not have to compete or endure the Third Born but must cope with the "you are too immature" message so becomes Fourth Born. The child following the Fourth Born feels alone because the Fourth Born ignores him or her.

These formative experiences occur around age two, sometimes even earlier. Relationships between siblings can change with time so that the early dynamics that formed the personalities are not apparent later.

For various reasons these circumstances can occur elsewhere in the order of children than where they are normally found. However, they will always be in sequence rather than occur randomly in a family. In other words, Second always follows First, Third always follows Second and so on.

BIRTH ORDER IN ART

DOES BIRTH ORDER affect how people enjoy art? Let's assume it does so we can imagine how they might enjoy art.

The Only Child likes to see things as they are. So, they would like realistic art that depicts things to which they can relate. They would like art that shows beautiful scenes, happy people, and animals. They want art that enables them to project into the art emotionally.

First Borns may be drawn to impressive art. They would probably favor large size artworks, amazing color combinations, and new, unexpected dimensions. They want awesome art.

Second Borns would probably like abstract art. They would tend to enjoy abstract art with lots of details that are not noticed when first viewed. They like art that can be interpreted, infused with meaning by the viewer, and enjoyed as a mental challenge.

Third Borns would probably like compassion in their art. They would relate to realistic art depicting human conditions that evoke sympathy, compassion, or understanding. They would like art that enables them to relate empathetically to the subject. They may also enjoy humor in their art.

Fourth Borns would probably like the darker side in art. Art that represents the world with mysterious threatening forces may speak to the Fourth experience of growing up in a world of older siblings who were threatening forces to the child. The Fourth would tend to relate to art that represents the mystical elements in life.

The artist him or herself may not create art that appeals to him or her according to Birth Order. Rather, the artist may tend to create art for someone else according to that person's Birth Order. If while growing up, it was important to please a Fourth Born the Second Born artist may create art to appeal to Fourth Borns. Though most artists appear to be Second Born, they can create any of the five types of art depending on whom they perceive their audience to be.

COMFORTING BY BIRTH ORDER

ONE READER RAISED the question of how Birth Order can help in comforting others in a time of grief. If you have comforted someone who has experienced a devastating loss, you know how difficult giving comfort can be. Sometimes we feel all we can do is give a hug.

The grieving person needs more than anything for someone to understand what he or she is going through. Sensing this, many people assure the grieving person, "I understand how you feel." Rather than comfort, this has the opposite effect because the person does not believe it. He or she thinks think there is no way for anyone to understand how they feel. And saying you understand suggests that you are not open to listening because you already understand.

The best way to prepare for comforting others is to understand Birth Order. Out of your understanding, you can make statements that truly comfort the other person. The person feels comforted when he or she senses you understand. You can produce this comfort if you understand the dynamics of grief according to Birth Order. It'll help you know what to say.

An Only experiences grief as chaos. Saying something like "This really devastates your world, doesn't it?" can be comforting.

A First Born experiences grief as a failure of love. Saying something like, "You really cared about him, didn't you?" can comfort the First Born.

A Second Born experiences grief as pain. Saying, "This really hurts, doesn't it?" can relieve grief.

A Third Born experiences grief as weakness as in "there was nothing I could do." Comfort can be given as "It's really hard to be strong right now, isn't it?"

A Fourth Born experiences grief as helplessness. You can comfort by saying "This really makes you feel helpless, doesn't it?"

Some people don't need comforting even though they have experienced a loss. These are the people who have had a good relationship with each other before death occurred. For them a wake or a funeral can actually be a celebration of life.

HOW DECISIONS ARE MADE BY BIRTH ORDER

WE LIVE BY the decisions we make. Our decisions can create problems when they are made without thinking, delayed too long, made for poor reasons, left up to others, made out of emotion such as anger, or made as a reaction to what someone else has done. Each Birth Order makes decisions differently so each has unique problems with decisions.

Only Children are the most likely to make decisions based on emotion. The emotion arises from how the new decision will affect the organization they have created in their lives. When they are called upon to make a decision, the first answer is most likely to be "no". After weighing the decision, the Only Child may change the "no" to a qualified "yes" because he or she has found a way to incorporate the decision into the structure he or she has developed. Since the Only Child decides on the basis of whether something fits, the Only may not think about the implications of the decision. A good question for an Only is to ask "Do I really want to do that even if I have time?"

First Borns tend to trust others more than themselves in making decisions. When someone the First Born trusts makes a suggestion, the First Born is apt to go along with it despite his or her own better judgment. Since the First Born knows more about his or her own situation than anyone else, someone else's suggestion may not fit the actual situation. Good people make bad decisions when they make them for someone else. The First Born needs to think about decisions rather than following suggestions carte blanche.

A Second Born makes decisions based on thinking, often only on thinking. In ignoring feelings, these decisions can be destructive to relationships and to one's own well-being. A Second Born may need to consciously consider how a decision is going to impact emotions. Sometimes it might be good for a Second Born to consult someone of another Birth Order to evaluate the emotional impact of a decision. The Second Born may feel trapped by making a decision that ignored feelings.

Third Borns can be compulsive about making decisions. They push others to make decisions and they push themselves to make decisions, often giving short shrift to thought that should go into making decisions. Consequently, the Third Born may often be putting out "fires" caused by the decisions he or she makes. The antidote for making rash decisions is to think about the impact that a decision makes on one's self and others. It is especially important to consider warnings by others.

Fourth Borns have the most difficulty with decisions. The Third Born during childhood pressures the Fourth Born to choose quickly so the Fourth Born tends to make decisions without thinking. These tend to be poor decisions that cause problems for the Fourth Born as well as others. The Fourth Born may, in fact, redo decisions frequently making it hard for people who rely on the Fourth Born. At other times the Fourth Born may think and think without reaching a decision. This can be difficult when a decision is required. The solution for the Fourth Born is to stop thinking about a decision once it is made. It is possible to do this if the decision is based on thinking beforehand.

Not all problems with making decisions are Birth Order based. Problem decisions can come from misinformation, lack of information, phobias, emotional pressure, deception, and other sources not related to Birth Order.

HOW BIRTH ORDER AFFECTS

CHRISTIAN SPIRITUALITY

BIRTH ORDER INFLUENCES the preferred type of spirituality of each personality. The features of each Birth Order can be seen in the spirituality of that person.

The Only Child is drawn to an ethical type of spirituality. In this spirituality, life's questions are answered, conclusions are drawn, and one's belief system is fixed. This spirituality includes a clear concept of right and wrong, clear definitions of the content of faith, and living life on the basis of the spirituality. It does not include a questioning of one's faith. This spirituality is organization with which the Only can live.

The First Born is drawn to the spirituality of the loving community. The First Born sees the validation of faith being in how the believer treats others, loves their enemies, creates a supportive community, turns the other cheek, and practices the Golden Rule. This spirituality addresses the First Born experience of living in a world lacking love.

The Second Born is drawn to a spirituality of self-discipline. The Second Born sees faith validated by the price persons are willing to pay for what they believe. The emphasis is on sacrifice, self-discipline, service, and commitment. This spirituality addresses the Second Born felt need to overcome the feelings of inadequacy.

The Third Born is drawn to a spirituality of

devotion with an emphasis on prayer, contact with God, spiritual experience, and the search for personal power through the Spirit of God. The Third Born is subconsciously overcoming the feeling of vulnerability through spirituality. The underlying purpose of this spirituality is to be strong.

The Fourth Born is drawn to mystical spirituality. The Fourth Born looks for God in life, discovery of what God is doing, the spiritual meaning of events, God's guidance, and the opportunity to analyze God's activity in life. This spirituality connects with the Fourth Born desire to be included, the drive to analyze, and the urge to probe the mysteries of life.

In the New Testament, the Gospels and Paul each represent one of these types of spirituality. The Only Child spirituality is expressed by the Gospel of Mark in the raising of questions that are answered by the reader. First Born spirituality is represented by Matthew with his emphasis on loving, particularly in the Sermon on the Mount. Luke expresses Second Born spirituality with his emphasis on taking up the cross to follow Jesus, the story of the prodigal son,and searching for the lost sheep through the night. John sets forth the Third Born devotional spirituality with the new birth, drawing power from Jesus like branches of a vine and an emphasis on redemption. Paul does mystical spirituality of the Fourth Born by constantly emphasizing the mysteries of life like seeing things through a dark glass.

Knowing how Birth Orders practice their spirituality may deliver you from judging someone to be deficient because their spirituality is different. Also, knowing the types of spirituality may enable you to expand your own spiritual experience with dimensions from the other Birth Orders.

Not all spirituality or claim to spirituality falls in these categories. There is a spirituality that rests on authority rather than experience. In this spirituality, there is a constant reference to authority whether it be a holy writing, a person, or a tradition. A cult represents an extreme form of this spirituality with its subservience to a cult leader. Spirituality that arises from trust in authority without reference to inner need may not be real spirituality.

BIRTH ORDER EMPATHY

IF YOU WANT empathy because you're feeling badly, what can you expect from each of the Birth Order personalities? You may not get the empathy you want. Here's why.

Each Birth Order has a different way of expressing empathy. An Only Child expresses empathy by talking about how you've been treated unfairly. A First Born expresses empathy by agreeing with you that you deserved better treatment. A Second Born expresses empathy by protecting a person from those who would make him or her feel inadequate. A Third Born expresses empathy by actually rescuing the person. A Fourth Born expresses empathy by attacking the system that victimizes a person.

Each Birth Order can withhold empathy as well. An Only Child withholds empathy when you have not done what you could. The First Born withholds empathy because you do not deserve better treatment. The Second Born withholds empathy if you are doing well otherwise. The Third Born withholds empathy if you turn down ideas on how to do better. The Fourth Born withholds empathy if there seems to be nothing wrong with the system to make you a victim.

INCREASING EFFECTIVE

INTELLIGENCE

A CLUE TO effective intelligence is found in Birth Order. We have found that the most intelligent person is the oldest child who is Third Born in personality. (See the chapter "A Super Intelligent Third Born") Knowing that Third Borns think by comparing, we realized that intelligence is the ability to compare things.

Every child begins life by constantly comparing new experiences with memories of past experiences. Consequently, children learn more in the first five years of life than they do in any other five-year period in their lives. If a child could continue this comparing, think how intelligent this child could be!

Unfortunately, comparing is stifled. When the child makes a comparison that is funny to others, like calling a rabbit a dog, the child experiences shame at being laughed at. At that point, the child becomes cautious about comparing so effective intelligence becomes limited. Before making a comparison, the child looks to see if it meets approval from others.

The child also learns to make comparisons aimed at things other than toward figuring things out. For example, Onlies compare how things are to how they expect them to be. First Borns compare their opinions to others' opinions. Second Borns compare what they do to what others do. Third Borns compare what others do to what they (others) could do. Fourth Born compare details to analyze. The energy used in making these comparisons limits effective intelligence for figuring things out.

In adult life, effective intelligence is limited when childhood memories of compulsive comparing are triggered. These memories are triggered whenever a person feels compelled to figure things out. The ability to compare is stifled just when a person needs it. To change this, we have your subconscious disconnect those compulsive memories of having to compare. So, say to yourself,

Forget the memories that make you compare.

Of course, you have often figured things out by making comparisons throughout your life. We want these memories to support your ability to compare so say to yourself,

Remember the memories that let you compare.

In about three days you should experience your mind being more active in processing what you are experiencing. Your awareness, focus, and creativity should all show improvement. Your effective intelligence will have been enhanced.

REVEALING HIDDEN INTELLIGENCE

EACH OF THE Birth Orders has its own way of thinking. Onlies organize, First Borns research, Second Borns evaluate, Third Borns compare, and Fourth Borns analyze. Each of these ways of thinking at some point brought negative reactions during childhood, making the children hide thinking patterns.

The Only might have been teased about organizing everything. The First Born might have been laughed at for quoting others. The Second Born might have been corrected for evaluating (criticizing) so much. The Third Born might have been told to stop comparing and the Fourth Born told to make up his or her mind. These reactions made a child hide thinking patterns not only from others but subconsciously from themselves.

These memories put a limit on intelligence. Sometimes this limit is experienced when a person looks back realizing that he or she had rejected a thought that should have been acknowledged. It restricts the use of intelligence.

Therapy for hiding thinking is to say to yourself, "Forget the memories that make you hide your thinking" to set thinking free. The other half of the therapy is "Remember the memories that let you hide your thinking" so you can keep thoughts to yourself when you know they will not be accepted.

WEDDING BEHAVIOR

BIRTH ORDER ENABLES us to figure out many things about the behavior of people. Recently someone emailed asking about the behavior of brides at their wedding. Here's what Birth Order reveals about this subject.

The Birth Order behavior is seen most clearly in brides who naturally see themselves as "special." The bride who is daddy's "little girl", who had older brothers who doted on her, or had a mother who gave her everything she wanted as well as protected her from life's demands learns to see herself as special. For her, the world exists to serve her but no one should expect anything of her.

In a wedding the bride is special. Everything centers on the bride. She's the one who is asked her preferences, is the central person in the wedding ceremony as she makes her entrance on her father's arm and the one who poses for the most pictures. If she is inclined by personality to see herself as special, she is in her element. In the wedding, the world is at her beck and call. How she acts out being special is determined by her Birth Order personality.

The Only Child bride who sees themselves as special insists on everything being right according to her standards. She must have the best photographer, the best gown, the best ceremony and the best reception. If things are not to her liking she expresses her exasperation with sighs, stamping her feet, crying, sarcastic cutting remarks, and outright shouting. Others may be surprised by her behavior in that happy setting. Parents may be embarrassed as they scramble about to meet her wishes, the groom may feel guilty at forgetting things, and her friends may get angry at those offending the bride.

The First Born bride who sees themselves as special reaches for the moon. She wants things that are out of reach. The ceremony must be an exceptionally impressive performance, the brides maids' dresses must be out of this world, the church must be decorated to the hilt, and the reception must have a meal to end all meals. When something falls short, there is no hiding her disappointment. While others may think the wedding was great, she knows it could have been better if others had just cooperated more.

The Second Born bride who sees themselves as special has to have every detail right. The bride's maids have to lose weight so they all look good. The groom has to learn how to walk just right down the aisle with her following the ceremony. The flower girl has to be trained endlessly to drop the flower petals just right. The people have to be seated in just the right places in just the right way by the right ushers. The food has to be served just right at the reception. And, the photographer must take just the right pictures - and woe to him if he misses a shot!

The Third Born bride who sees themselves as special has to be treated just right by everyone. Her feelings must always be considered without her having to ask. People must ask her if she is comfortable, if she needs a glass of water, if the organization of the ceremony suits her, if she has what she needs in the dressing room, if the temperature is just right, or if the lighting bothers her. As the bride feeling special, she must have everyone concerned about how she is feeling. If this solicitousness is lacking, she feels cheated. This is her day! Everyone must care about her today.

The Fourth Born bride who sees themselves as special must be the center of attention at all times. She feels irritated, even angry, when the groom is asked for an opinion without her being included. She is upset if the bride's maids get together without her being there. She is offended if the groom talks to someone else without including her. She is jealous if her mother gets attention instead of her, if everyone takes attention off of her to laugh at a humorous remark made by a bride's maid at the rehearsal, or if the photographer pays attention to how the others are posing instead of to her. She may be angry much of the time at her own wedding.

The bride who is human instead of "special" appreciates all that is done for her. She enjoys the attention given to her, overlooks things that are not perfect, wants everyone to enjoy the occasion, and pays attention to people often sidelined - older guests, children, and people who have traveled great distances. She enjoys expressing her love toward her groom, giving gifts to the participants in the wedding party, and talking about plans for the future. She gets excited opening gifts, expressing her joy profusely. She makes others feel good.

For more on couples' relationships read, "The Birth Order Effect for Couples".

BIRTH ORDER RITE OF PASSAGE

THE BIRTH ORDERS make a decision in early childhood that keeps them behaving like children in adult life. By making the right decision, a person goes from childhood to adulthood in a rite of passage.

Since the Only Child experiences being alone so much in childhood, the Only decides that "When I grow up I will not let anyone leave me." This leads the Only to keep people from leaving by continuing to talk as the other person wants to get away. The Only may plead for someone to stay or invite the person to look at one more thing before they leave. The rite of passage decision for the Only is "It's okay for someone to leave me." This allows the Only to accept the reality that there is always a time to part.

The First Born having experienced mother turning away to take care of the baby, decides "When I grow up I'm not going to let anyone reject me." The First Born becomes agreeable, passive, and non-assertive to avoid giving others reasons to reject him or her. The rite of passage decision is "It's okay for someone to reject me." This allows the First Born to accept rejection as a normal part of life rather than something to feel bad about.

The Second Born having experienced the First Born taking attention away, decides "When I grow up I am not going to let anyone do better than I can." This decision leads to competitiveness, perfectionism, and attention to detail to avoid losing someone's attention. The rite of

210

passage decision is "It's okay for someone to do better than I can." In the real world, there are always people who can do better than you can but you're still okay.

The Third Born having experienced pressure from the Second Born outdoing him or her, decides "When I grow up I'm not going to let anyone corner me." This decision leads the Third Born to become fearless, take risks, and seek alternatives to avoid being cornered. The rite of passage decision is "It's okay for someone to corner me" so that the fear of being cornered is not an issue as it was in childhood. The adult has choices the child does not so is not cornered.

The Fourth Born experiences being trapped when told by the Third Born "you're not big enough, strong enough, etc. to play with us." This leads to the Fourth having commitment phobia, becoming perpetually angry or passive or getting involved in conflict to avoid being trapped. The rite of passage decision is "It's okay for someone to trap me" so that the fear of being trapped is not an issue. A child with very limited choices is trapped but the adult has options that allow the adult to be free.

A good way to use these rite of passage decisions with others is to include them as a thought for the day at the end of an email.

BIRTH ORDERS CONTROLLING OTHERS

ALL OF US are controlled as we grow up, controlled by parents, older siblings, members of the family, our school teachers, and even playmates. Control becomes an issue that gets expressed according to our Birth Order. Our programming makes us try to control others.

Onlies try to control what others do. They do it by giving advice, telling others what to do, and by reacting emotionally to what others do. This form of control is rooted in having an early childhood imaginary companion who, of course, was controlled by the Only. This companion did exactly as directed by the Only Child. The controlling Only expects others to do what they're told and that can work well in management or teaching school.

First Borns try to control others by getting them to agree. To do this, First Borns explain things while nodding their heads to signal agreement. This form of control comes from the First Born being held accountable for the behavior of younger siblings, parents demanding an explanation of how something happened. The First Born had to explain and explaining became a way of life even when explaining is unnecessary. The original explaining was to get parents to agree to the First Born version of things. First Borns look for the explanation of things making them research thinkers.

Second Borns try to control others' thinking. To do this, they feed others selected facts to make others think a certain way. This comes from discovering in childhood the power of giving parents facts to demolish the First Born's explanations that made the Second Born look bad. The Second Born did not try to out-explain the First Born, just use a fact or two. The "facts" didn't have to be true. Also, the Second Born did not give other facts that would make the Second Born look bad. This programming makes the Second Born into a rational thinker.

Third Borns try to control others by persuading them to change their strategies. To do this, they try to scare others or they try to entice others to adopt a particular strategy. They learned to do this coping with the Second Born who was using facts to control. Not being able to counter the Second Born control with explanations or with facts, they tried to persuade the Second Born to change strategies. As adults, Third Borns can be quite persuasive, enabling them often to be the best of sales people.

Fourth Borns try to control others to keep them from doing what they want. To do this, they can intimidate or manipulate, intimidate through anger and manipulate by playing victim. They learned to do this coping with the Third Born who did not share facts with them while trying to make them adopt strategies that often turned out badly for the Fourth Born. The Fourth Born could only counter the Third Born strategies by getting angry or by withdrawing into a passive victim role. Fourth Borns using anger and manipulation have difficulty relating to others so they tend to isolate socially. However, since the Third Born did not give facts the Fourth Born learned to look for clues that often give insight into what is going on in a situation.

Fortunately, most people overcome their tendencies to control others in adult life. This happens when experiencing others who refuse to be controlled. The more freedom we grant to others the better relationships we have. Feedback we give to others encourages them to give up their controlling ways.

RAISING OBNOXIOUS CHILDREN

YOUR BIRTH ORDER may cause you to raise obnoxious kids, regardless of your Birth Order. Your Birth Order may cause you unconsciously to reward obnoxious behavior that reinforces that behavior.

If you are an Only, you may be giving in to obnoxious behavior simply to stop the child from fussing. If you are a First Born, you may want to be nice to your child even when the child is not being nice to you. If you are a Second, you may want to create peace so you give in to the child to calm things down. If you are a Third, you may want to please the child when he or she is ranting. If you are a Fourth, you may want to buddy up to your child when the child is being obnoxious.

All of these behaviors reward the obnoxious behavior of the child. The child learns to repeat the behavior to get the desired effect from you, the parent. So, what do you do?

The best response from the parent is one that challenges the child. A child loves to be challenged. Watch a small child at play in the yard. The child is constantly looking for challenges. They look for things to climb, things to pull themselves up on, things to throw, things to lift, things to roll, and things to experiment with. When children get older they seek challenges in sports, video games, and contests with friends. The love of challenges never goes away.

Believe it or not, children rise to a challenge from

214

you the parent. Issuing a challenge can produce the effect you want. That's a challenge for you, isn't it?

A challenge is issued following the words "Can you....?" Angry parents often present this challenge in a tone of voice that makes things worse. The words need to be said with the tone of voice, demeanor, and gestures that make it a challenge rather than a confrontation.

The challenge should get what you want from the child. If you want the child to be quiet, ask the child "Can you wait for five minutes?" setting the timer so the child knows when the time is up. Then, reward the child the way you did when he was raising a fuss. The child learns to get what he wants from you in a way that pleases you.

If you want the child to pick up toys ask, "Can you pick up your toys?" When the child does then give the reward that you used to give for the bad behavior. If you want the child to be considerate ask, "Can you be nice to Grandma when she comes over?" rewarding the child with the kind of attention you gave previously during that tantrum phase.

Never reward the anti-social obnoxious behavior. Ignore it if you can. Issue the right kind of challenge if you can. If nothing works you might want to get professional help.

The greatest obstacles will come from your own Birth Order. As an Only, you may be unable to tolerate your child being upset. Decide that it is okay for you to feel okay when your child feels bad.

As a First Born, your Birth Order may create guilt at your child experiencing any discomfort. Decide that it is okay for you to feel okay when your child is angry at you.

As a Second Born, you may find it hard to resist creating peace when you child continues in hostile behavior. Decide it is okay for you to okay when your child wants to engage in conflict.

As a Third Born, you may have an intense desire to

please your child. It hurts inside to see your child put on the crying scene. Allow yourself to feel okay when your child appears to be sad.

As a Fourth Born, you may feel rejected by your child when he or she cries out "I hate you." Let yourself feel okay when your child screams at you.

Life will be better for you, your child, and the whole family when you issue challenges to your child rather than cave in to emotional blackmail. This is your challenge! See how good it feels?!

COMMITMENT PHOBIA AND
BIRTH ORDER

I WANT TO share some thoughts with you about commitment phobia (CP) and Birth Order. First, let me define CP as I understand it. CP is the fear of being trapped. A parent may create the phobia saying to a child "you made your bed, you lie in it." In other words, the parent is saying you are stuck with whatever choice you have made. There is no remaking your bed. That's scary!

Any Birth Order can experience CP. A person can be indecisive to avoid making a commitment, anxious having made a commitment, or constantly looking for a way to relieve the pressure of commitment. It can make a person continually change jobs or become unhappy in a job after a short time. It can make a person buy impulsively to act before the phobia puts a stop to it. It also affects marriages.

I have observed CP especially in Fourth Born/Second Born marriages. They express their CP differently. The Fourth Born seeks to overcome the phobia while the Second Born is resigned to being trapped. These marriages can last for decades before they break up.

The married Fourth Born (and others with CP) may relieve the sense of being trapped with an affair or affairs. Or, the Fourth Born may fill life with work so there is little time for family relationships that would trigger CP. One Fourth Born man tried to escape CP by sleeping in a

217

different part of the house. A woman simply would not eat with the family but retreated to her bedroom to eat.

He or she may also sabotage the relationship to escape feeling trapped. By making the relationship difficult, the Fourth Born with CP feels freer than in a good relationship. To make things hard, the Fourth Born disagrees with everything because agreement would trigger CP. The Fourth Born can be in a constant state of anger, continually complaining, or non-communicative to keep from feeling trapped. To have a pleasant conversation, to reach agreement, or even to cooperate would be to suffer from CP. Some avoid CP by controlling their partners, keeping them from doing what they want or from having money that would enable them to be free. When the partner feels miserable, the Fourth Born feels free of CP. Some Fourth Born men feel so comfortable when the wife is weeping that they want to have sex with her at that time.

Second Borns married to Fourth Borns are resigned to being trapped. Instead of fighting to overcome CP, they submit to it. They endure the control, go along with the Fourth Born behavior, and keep their feelings hidden from others and themselves. They don't like it but they stay in it. The breakup comes when something tips the scales for the Second Born. A woman may inherit some money that enables her to leave, the Fourth Born may do something intolerably outrageous, or a crisis occurs that makes the Second Born realize it's time to get out. The Second Born is the one to leave the marriage. When the Second Born leaves, the Fourth Born is taken by surprise because the Fourth Born did not experience the marriage as bad. Once out, there is no going back for the Second Born. They are just as committed to staying out as they were to staying in.

If a phobic Fourth Born is married to an Only, the Fourth Born, male or female, can be abusive to the Only. An Only is a fixer who wants the other person to be happy. The Only counters whatever bad thing the Fourth Born does or says with something good in order to improve the relationship. If the Fourth Born complains about the meal, the Only changes it. If the Fourth Born is angry about what the Only did, the Only will redo it. If the Fourth Born is angry, the Only tries to satisfy. The Only tries hard to overlook whatever destructive things the Fourth Born does in order to make the relationship better. The Fourth Born may get so frustrated with the Only trying to make things better that he or she can get violent. In these relationships, the police are involved over and over as violence gets out of hand. Onlies can be so optimistic about fixing relationships that the police are called seven times on average before a woman leaves the relationship.

CP is about feeling trapped. The alternative to feeling trapped is to feel free. Here is a thought that can relieve CP: Forget making yourself be free, just let yourself be free. This thought can work wonders in a relationship troubled with CP. Share it with people who are suffering CP.

BIRTH ORDER BODY LANGUAGE

IDENTIFICATION OF BIRTH Order personality can be done through body language. Elements of each personality are expressed non-verbally in ways that reveal that personality.

Feelings are communicated non-verbally through facial expressions by the Only Child, with feelings expressed by the eyes, head movements, and mouth. Hand movements, gestures, and voice inflections accompany the Only Child's verbal communication.

Head nodding, a questioning look including furrowed brow, looking at you when you're talking but looking away when he or she is talking indicate First Born. The words "I don't know" are sprinkled in the conversation as well as pauses punctuated by "ah" or "um" showing the tentative nature of First Born communication in which the First Born would rather know what you think rather than express a possibly offensive opinion. The head nodding is to convey agreement for the sake of the relationship rather than a considered opinion.

A piercing look, crisp language, upright posture marks the Second Born. Facial expression can be dramatic but is a studied expression rather than the free expression of the Only Child, a skill often developed in the teens during long hours in front of the mirror. Language is often punctuated by the words "need" or "have to" as in "You need to…" or "You have to…." Anger often lies just beneath the surface in the Second Born especially if the

Second Born had an older First Born sibling of the same sex.

Laughter, a joking manner, and pushiness can mark the Third Born. Body movements are spontaneous rather than controlled as in the Second Born. Conversation can be spontaneous often taking a new direction unexpectedly. In conversation, the Third Born often responds with a better idea, or a new direction, or an improvement to whatever you have said, giving you the impression the Third Born wants to think for you.

A chameleon like response marks the Fourth Born who has practiced many types of personalities in childhood and perhaps in adulthood. After the first few moments of conversation, the Fourth Born will have adapted to communication with you. During those first few minutes of conversation, you feel the Fourth Born is truly interested in you as the Fourth Born studies you to know how to interact with you. One common facial characteristic is that the mouth is more expressive than the eyes. Feelings are seen in movements of the mouth, lips and jaw rather than the eyes. The Fourth Born voice tends to be softer in some Fourth Borns and louder than normal in others. The soft voice indicates giving up on being heard and the loud voice on forcing a hearing. The Fourth Born can violate personal space by getting too close, by touching, or by making inappropriate remarks. Or, the Fourth Born can be shy, reclusive, quiet, and withdrawn.

Recognizing another's Birth Order early is an advantage in communication. Knowing a person's Birth Order lets you have an understanding of the personality so that pitfalls can be avoided. Also, observing Birth Order expressed non-verbally makes people-watching more fun.

BIRTH ORDER CONTROL

WE ARE BORN helpless. We have no control over ourselves or our environment. Gradually we gain control so that we can hold the rattle, roll over, and pull ourselves up. Getting control becomes a major goal in life. It shows up in Birth Order behavior.

The Only Child wants to control space, time, and things in resistance to interference by helpful parents and others in the Only Child's activity. The helpful adult rearranges things, changes the space by removing or adding things, and rushes the child rather than giving time. Even in adult life the person feels compelled to control time, space, and things. The Only resists being interrupted, lays claim to his or her own space, and maintains his or her own schedule. The Only feels frustrated when unable to control his or her own environment.

The First Born feels the need to control others' opinions about him or her. Having "lost" mother's love to the baby the First Born looks for ways to get it back by being good, showing off, or doing what mother wants. This becomes a lifelong pattern of catering to others' emotions to get them to feel good toward the First Born. The First Born feels guilty if others show signs of displeasure toward him or her.

The Second Born, in the face of First Born behavior, wants to control that behavior. The Second Born feels the need to keep the First Born from showing off and to make the First Born look bad in the competition for mother's love. In adult life, the Second Born may feel compelled to control others by making rules, offering criticisms, or by competing with others. When the Second Born is unable to control another's behavior he or she experiences anger.

As a child, the Third Born experiences Second Born control and tries to counter it with new, better ideas. In adult life, the Third Born tries to control others' thinking by overriding their ideas, often becoming pushy with others. On a positive note, they may contribute ideas liberally without trying to smother another's ideas. When they are unable to control another's ideas they can become stubborn in reacting to this person.

The Fourth Born feels overwhelmed by older siblings, especially the Third Born, whom he or she would like to control. In trying to achieve control the Fourth Born may develop strategies for sabotaging the older siblings' behavior by lying, tattling, accusing, throwing tantrums, or acting like a victim. In adult life, the Fourth Born can be emotionally and/or physically controlling, manipulative and threatening. The Fourth Born may also seek to control others by playing victim with a "poor me" message. When the Fourth Born is unable to control someone he or she may become vengeful.

Each of the Birth Orders can practice internal controlling as well. The Only controls self by thinking that life is full of things you "have to" do so that he or she does not get to do what he or she "wants" to do. The First Borns control their own thinking/feeling in order to not offend someone else. Second Borns control themselves by hiding their feelings in order to better control others' behavior. Third Borns control themselves by trying to do away with their fears in order to be free to challenge others' thinking. Fourth Borns suppress their feelings so they do not interfere with controlling others.

To minimize controlling each Birth Order has its

own challenge. Onlies are challenged to enjoy life even when it becomes chaotic. First Borns are challenged to accept feedback from others rather than try to influence it. Second Borns are challenged to enjoy others' successes. Third Borns are challenged to appreciate others' ideas. Fourth Borns are challenged to enjoy people as they are. Meeting these challenges enhances life, relieves the stress of having to control, and lets one be free to use energy for living life rather than for controlling.

COMPASSION DEFICIT DISORDER

IT'S A PLEASURE to talk with people who care about how you feel. The pleasure comes from being understood, supported, accepted, or, in other words, from compassion. On the other hand, there are those who turn away when you start to talk about personal feelings, who want to fix problems rather than listen, who want to think for you by giving advice, who want to talk about themselves rather than pay attention to you, and who quickly find someone else to chat with. This is the failure of compassion.

No one is completely without compassion but it may be limited by childhood memories. The memories that limit compassion are memories of being made to feel bad as a child. As we were made to feel bad and unable to figure out how to feel better, we decided that when we grew up we would not let anyone make us feel bad. This decision, stored in our subconscious, impairs our ability to feel compassion.

In adult life, this decision helps us when someone wants to make us feel bad. We shrug off insults, insinuations, put-downs, criticisms, etc. designed to create bad feelings. We are protecting ourselves from bad feelings. However, bad feelings also come from someone who is sharing their bad feelings with us and we protect ourselves from those feelings as well. Protecting ourselves from those feelings is Compassion Deficit Disorder (CDD).

Each of the Birth Orders has its own version of CDD. The Only Child CDD is an organizing response to bad feelings in which the Only tells you to do something different. The First Born CDD is explaining something or someone rather than listening to your feelings – you're not ready to understand someone else when you're feeling bad. The Second Born may tell you to quit feeling bad because that's the way it is. The Third Born jumps to a conclusion on how your problem can be solved without listening to how you feel. The Fourth Born may either comfort you without understanding your pain or get angry in a close relationship.

Since CDD is subconscious, it requires therapy that reaches the subconscious. Memories in the subconscious that drive CDD are compulsive/obsessive in that they require you to feel bad but do not allow you to feel bad. You were made to feel bad in childhood but were not allowed to feel bad. Therapy neutralizes those memories to set you free from having to feel bad. On the other hand, feeling bad for someone is good so you want to reinforce memories that allow you to feel bad to have compassion. To use this therapy in a statement, say out loud to yourself, "Forget making yourself feel bad, just let yourself feel bad." Letting yourself feel bad lets you have compassion for someone else who is feeling bad.

Actually, the effects of compassion therapy are broader than just feeling for someone who is feeling bad. Compassion enables a person to respond to a wide range of feelings to enrich relationships. All relationships such as marriage, raising children, family, friendship, working with others, doing business, benefit from compassion. When you have compassion others can read it in your face, voice, and actions.

THE BARRIER OF ANGER

WOULD YOU LIKE for your relationship to be free of anger? Anger in a relationship makes you feel helpless, take on the victim role, and causes pain. We have learned to fear anger as children and that fear is still with us. To feel safe, we do what we can to hide from it, pacify the person who is angry, or get angry ourselves before the other person can get angry. The anger puts a wedge between us, drives away people with whom we want to be close and attracts people to us who want to fight.

Let's assume that something can be done to get rid of anger.

Anger destroys relationships. Anger causes conflict, scares children as well as spouse, and leads to destructive behavior. Hidden anger communicated to others makes them be cautious around you. Others try to feel safe by hiding their feelings from you, trying to pacify you, or by preempting your anger by getting angry first. To improve relationships, you need to lose that anger.

We often communicate anger with no awareness that we are doing so non-verbally though the sound of our voices, the look in our eyes, the expression on our faces, the gestures we make, and a multitude of other signals. This non-verbal communication of anger is not only a turnoff but it invites others to be angry at you. Frequent anger at you may be a sign that you are subconsciously displaying anger to others.

The non-verbal component is the majority of our

communication. Non-verbal messages comprise 93% while words contribute just 7% of our communication with the non-verbal part being beyond our control. Even if we control our tone of voice, facial expression or gestures there is still much that we communicate without knowing it. To stop communicating anger, we need to deal with the sources of anger. It's not enough to manage our anger.

Understanding Birth Order connections to anger can alleviate anger because each Birth Order has its own kind of anger. Awareness of anger dynamics can enable a person to dissociate from that anger through looking at it objectively.

The Only Child experiences anger as frustration. When the Only is unable to control circumstances he/she may get angry at being frustrated. There is an unconscious expectation that somehow anger will make things work better. Realizing anger won't fix anything may enable the Only to give up that anger in favor of more constructive ways of overcoming chaos.

The First Born feels entitled to respect that, when it is not forthcoming, makes the First Born angry. The desire for respect is rooted in a deeper desire for love and is a substitute for it. To dissociate from that anger, the First Born needs to recognize that anger is not going to get love nor will it earn him/her respect. The First Born needs to know it is okay to have respect and the way to get it is to show love rather than rage.

The Second Born gets angry when he/she perceives that no one cares about his/her feelings. Of course, anger is ineffective in making others sensitive to the Second Born's feelings. Rather, it makes others think that the Second Born does not care about anyone else's feelings. The Second Born needs to see that being emotionally open is more likely to encourage others to care about his/her feelings than anger which makes people defensive.

The Third Born generates ideas that he/she wants

others to value. When others ignore these ideas, go with other ideas, or simply reject them, the Third Born gets angry. The Third Born needs to know it is okay to desire others to consider your ideas. However, if the Third Born understands that anger does not attract people to ideas, he /she may be able to let go of anger to find other strategies to get his/her ideas considered.

The Fourth Born is the most likely of all the Birth Orders to experience anger in relationships because he/she was not valued by the older siblings. The Fourth Born feeling unwanted can get angry and, since anger drives others away, he/she continues to feel unwanted and angry. Realizing that anger will not attain what he/she wants the Fourth Born may be able to give it up in favor of better strategies for relating with people. Getting rid of the anger allows for closer relationships.

This can be a good start for disposing of the anger that interferes with relationships. However, it may not take care of all the anger. Memories of past experiences, when triggered, can be a source of anger beyond Birth Order. To deal with these sources of anger, a person needs to deal with the memories so they no longer produce the anger. This may require professional help or it may be accomplished by talking to someone who is patient, understanding, and able to listen thoughtfully.

Your reward is better relationships that happen effortlessly after the barrier of anger is gone.

COMMUNICATION BIRTH ORDER STYLE

VERBAL COMMUNICATION HAPPENS on two levels, information and meaning. It is helpful for communication to distinguish the two, especially as they are used by Birth Order.

Before we look at the Birth Order connection, let's look at communication itself.

Communication of information comes by talking and listening. The talker tells something and the listener takes in the information. Sounds simple, doesn't it? But there can be obstacles to talking and listening. A common obstacle to talking comes from memories of being told to not interrupt when someone's talking, memories that can now keep a person from telling something. Difficulty with listening comes from memories of having to endure lectures that made the child stop listening, memories that cause an adult to not hear what someone is saying.

Communicating meaning requires more than talking and listening, it requires explaining and understanding. The person who explains conveys meaning and the other who understands grasps the meaning. Explaining is made difficult by memories of being made to explain in self-defense as a child, memories that make adults revert to defending themselves rather than explaining so others can understand. Understanding is blocked by memories of being angrily confronted with a stern, "Do you understand?" These memories make the adult jump to conclusions rather than listening to a complete explanation.

Two affirmations can improve communication: "Never get so interested in talking that you forget to listen" and "Never get so interested in explaining that you forget to understand." Through the subconscious these affirmations enable a person to talk, listen, explain, and understand more clearly.

Now, let's go on to the Birth Order issues. When acting out of Birth Order, here's how each communicates meaning in relation to facts:

The Only Child communicates facts that hide meaning in a form I call meta-communication. Rather than say what he or she means, the Only makes a factual statement that suggests the hidden meaning that, because it is hidden, is subject to being misunderstood. For example, when the room is warm the Only might say "What's the temperature in here?" rather than "I'm feeling uncomfortable with the heat." The hearer is supposed to understand the meaning which is to turn down the thermostat without being told explicitly.

The First Born is cautious about sharing meaning, wanting instead to know the meaning others put to facts. For instance, the First Born might say "I wonder why it so warm in here?" to get you to come up with a meaning for the temperature. The First Born tends not to draw meaning from factual information but waits for the other person to put the meaning in. This trait makes First Borns ready to believe what others say.

The Second Born wants to talk facts, not meaning. Rather than explain things, Second Borns will give factual details so that meaning should be self-evident. For example, in dealing with the room being warm, the Second Born can talk about how much it costs to overheat a room, how it is healthier to have a lower temperature, how a person can always put on a sweater if they're uncomfortable with the temperature, and how a person can get used to a lower temperature. With enough details, the Second Born believes the other person will understand that the thermostat should be turned down. However, the person may misunderstand the meaning so that he or she feels criticized for being so thoughtless as to have the room be too warm.

The Third Born thinks about meaning while giving short shrift to facts. Thus, the Third Born is the most likely to jump to conclusions. If the temperature is too high in the room, the Third Born may inquire about your health thinking that's why you have the heat so high. Since the Third Born starts with meaning rather than facts, you don't know if it's the temperature, your pale complexion, or something else that makes the Third Born think you are not feeling well. The Third Born may come across as pushy as he or she comes up with interpretations as to why the temperature is so high.

The Fourth Born is apt to put his or her own meaning into facts. So, when the room is too warm, the Fourth Born may take that to mean that the host does not want the Fourth Born to stay long. In fact, the Fourth Born may get angry at the host for the high temperature and is certain that his or her interpretation is right. By putting their own meaning into facts, Fourth Borns can seem out of touch with reality, interpreting things in such a way that others pull back from them.

In summary, Onlies hide meaning, Firsts seek meaning, Seconds reject meaning, Thirds impose meaning, and Fourths create meaning. Keeping these differences in mind can enhance your ability to communicate with people according to Birth Order.

CONNECTING THE DOTS

YOU HAVE ALL heard the expression "connecting the dots." Connecting the dots is just one way of processing dots but not the only way. There are several other ways Birth Orders process dots.

The Only personality processes dots by arranging them. Arranging dots means scheduling, planning, making lists, sorting, placing things in the correct places, or making assignments. The Only's natural urge to organize drives the arranging of dots. To be comfortable, an Only must put dots in order.

The First Born collects dots. When someone shares an idea, an insight, an observation, a comparison, or an opinion the First Born eagerly receives it. However, the First Born may not do much beyond collecting the dots. The dots are not connected, arranged, compared, or evaluated. Rather, they are passed on to others who will listen. Craving love moves the First Born to collect and share dots. The sharing of dots feels like an expression of love – someone cared enough for me to tell me something.

The First Born may overwhelm the Second Born with dots. Growing up, the Second Born cannot compete in collecting dots with the First Born because the First Born has a head start. And, the perfectionist Second Born is not satisfied with collecting dots, he or she must connect dots. In connecting dots, the Second Born forms a structure from the dots, a box if you will. Having made the box, the Second Born is comfortable thinking within that box. Any new dots to be accepted have to be connected with dots in the structure. Communicating with others includes imposing a box or boxes on them.

The Third Born chafes under the strictures of the Second Born box. Accepting the box would be safe thinking for the Third Born but, needing to challenge fear, the Third Born has to think outside the box. So, the Third Born creates new dots. That's where the Third Born finds adventure. When the Second Born compels the Third Born to accept boxes, the Third Born gets pushy in response. The Third Born may expand the strategy to push others, a characteristic with which the Fourth Born must cope.

The Fourth Born doesn't always cave in to the Third Born. The Fourth Born may be determined to think for himself or herself rather than accept Third Born dots. Of course, the Fourth Born resistance makes the Third Born push harder until the Fourth Born decides he or she must erase those Third Born dots in order to think. As an adult, the Fourth Born may react to what others say as if they were trying to think for him or her, erasing dots wherever they come from. To erase dots, the Fourth Born may reject the dots, disagree, criticize, get angry, ignore dots or very frequently, try to confuse things. Erasing dots makes for difficult communication because thoughts are not accepted. For this Fourth Born relationships are hard to maintain.

Fortunately, Birth Order characteristics usually mellow with life experience. This means that Onlies come to accept some chaos, First Borns learn to evaluate dots, Second Borns become more flexible, Third Borns ease up to become more considerate, and Fourth Borns accept others' thoughts more readily. But, the Birth Order ways of processing dots are still apparent if you pay attention.

In summary,
Onlies arrange dots
First Borns collect dots

Second Borns connect dots
Third Borns create dots
Fourth Borns erase dots

Once you recognize how each Birth Order processes dots you can recognize Birth Order personality more easily. You learn to appreciate the creativity that each uses in the processing of dots. More importantly, by understanding your own processing of dots, you get beyond your Birth Order behavior pattern.

BIRTH ORDER AND A.D.D.

ATTENTION DEFICIT DISORDER is a very common thinking disorder. Almost everyone experiences ADD (Attention Deficit Disorder) to some degree. If you want to know if you have it, these are the signs of ADD:

1. Your mind goes blank during a conversation.
2. You have to read something several times to get it.
3. You have trouble sleeping because you cannot stop thinking.

How do you get ADD? Some think it to be genetic but I have found that ADD goes back to an experience(s) at around age two when you thought with your whole body. Your thinking and doing was the same thing for you. It was similar to what you experience in a crisis when you act and think in unison. In a crisis, you do not have time to separate the two. In normal situations, you can separate your thinking from your actions.

As a two-year-old you explore your world sometimes getting into trouble in the process. You pull down the drapes, draw a crayon mural on the dining room wall or pull the table cloth off the table, dishes and all. The most patient of parents is apt to get pushed too far so that you get punished, reprimanded, isolated, or otherwise made to know your parent's displeasure. You get scared. You don't want that to happen again so you have to figure out what you did wrong.

You think about what you did. Since you cannot separate thinking from acting, you decide you got into trouble for thinking. In your own way, you decided that sometimes it is dangerous to think. This decision became a memory that hinders your thinking. When that memory is activated, your subconscious halts your thinking to protect you from getting punished for thinking.

Your ADD kicks in when you feel you **have** to think. When you feel that you have to think, the memories are triggered causing your subconscious to react by saying "Oh, oh, it's dangerous to think" and turn off your thinking. This shutdown occurs during a conversation where your thinking is challenged so that you cannot respond. The shutdown also occurs when you read something that requires you to think, making you read it several times before you get it.

On the other hand, during the night when you are safe in your bed in the darkness and silence of night, your subconscious lets you know that it is safe to think. At night, when you should be sleeping you are thinking. During the day when you should be thinking, your mind goes blank. That's ADD.

Since each Birth Order has its own thinking style the ADD effect is unique to each:

Only Child the organizing thinker: Organizing becomes a distraction to thinking. For example, the supervisor behind the desk might be putting things in order on his desk rather than thinking about what an employee is explaining to him. At night, the Only thinks about tomorrow's schedule, issues that have to be dealt with, or things that have to be done.

First Born the researcher: Research becomes the distraction for thinking. With ADD, the First Born thinks about things he wants to find out rather than thinking about what he is being told or what he is reading at the moment.

During the night he may lie awake figuring things out.

Second Born the evaluator: ADD would drive the Second Born into thinking about irrelevant details rather than the issue at hand. During the night, ADD drives the person into evaluating projects, people, and situations rather than sleeping.

Third Born the associative thinker: With ADD, this person thinks about different situations rather than thinking about what she is hearing or reading. During the night, this person lies awake making comparisons.

Fourth Born the analyzer: ADD makes the Fourth Born ask "what if" questions to stop thinking about what is being said or what he or she is reading. During the night, this person lies awake analyzing events, conversations, and situations compulsively.

The words "Forget making yourself think, just let yourself think" can be used as therapy for ADD. You can say this to yourself or to a child who struggles with ADD. You might want to post this statement on your refrigerator as a reminder to reinforce the therapy. On the subconscious level, the statement sets you free to think during the day and allows you to stop thinking during the night so you can sleep.

THE EFFECT OF ABUSE

ABUSE IS THE punitive treatment a child receives when wanting love. An example would be when the three-year-old drops a vase that breaks into pieces. At that moment of unexpected disaster, the child craves understanding, compassion, forgiveness, and acceptance that affirms the child as more important than the vase. In other words, the child craves love and needs love at that moment because the child had an accident. Instead, the child may receive a reprimand, a spanking, an expression of disappointment, or a verbal thrashing. The child gets abuse when expecting love. Thus love connects with abuse.

This childhood memory sets up a compulsive/obsessive memory pattern that makes the person subconsciously expect abusive treatment when craving love. To fulfill this expectation, the person may connect with people who are abusive, misinterpret what others say, do or express emotionally as abusive, and may do things to invite abuse. An example of interpreting good behavior as abuse would be the man who comes home to find his wife has made fried chicken for supper instead of the pork chops he expected. Because he had his mind set on pork chops, he sees her serving fried chicken as abuse that justifies his anger toward her. So he berates her, knocks the dishes to the floor, and may even batter her.

Each of the Birth Orders has a different reaction to what they see as abuse. The Only Child responds to abuse by withdrawing into a private world where they react angrily to intrusion. The First Born is the most likely to sulk when they feel abused as a withdrawal of love similar to what they experienced in the loss of love to the Second Born. The Second Born is likely to criticize when feeling abused because criticism is a way to make the other person feel inadequate. The Third Born is likely to attack because, feeling vulnerable, the best defense is a good offense. Having three older siblings, the Fourth Born often experiences the greatest amount of abuse from siblings and parents so tends to see many behaviors as abuse that justifies retaliatory behavior to punish the abusers.

The scenario of love being confused with abuse can be changed. Recognizing the power of memories to make you feel like the whole world is abusive is the first step to gaining freedom from this effect. When recalling childhood experiences of abuse, it is useful to tell yourself to forget those memories. Your subconscious will listen to you to disconnect those memories so they lose their power over you. The next step is to put a positive spin on what others communicate. Third, realize that others are struggling with the memories that make them touchy so that you can interpret their behavior as being their problem rather than taking it personally.

To recover, Onlies need to realize that interruption is not abuse. First Borns need to realize that attention paid to others does not constitute abuse. Second Borns need to know that someone else getting praise does not mean abuse. Third Borns need to know that someone doing something their own way does not mean abuse. Fourth Borns need to know that disagreement is not abuse.

Lots of things can happen when you perceive love instead of abuse in the people around you. They become more friendly, you live more confidently rather than defensively, you use your energy positively rather than negatively, and you enjoy life itself more.

BIRTH ORDER IN THE CLASSROOM

TEACHING CAN BE challenging as children act out their birth order personalities in the classroom. Birth order suggests certain strategies that can help minimize negative behavior, encourage children to learn more effectively, and create positive attitudes.

Understanding birth order may not be a top priority for busy teachers nor does it have to be. Some strategies based on birth order can be used without knowing the full extent of birth order personality. Of course, knowing birth order itself can enhance teacher/student relationships, communication, and insights into behavior.

The following strategies can make a big difference in a classroom. Even though these can be used with the whole class, they are not one-size-fits-all. Each one of these applies to a different birth order. Students of other birth orders are affected little or not at all by strategies meant for one birth order so they can be used with the whole class. Each will take from it what he or she needs.

These strategies are as follows:

1. Only child: Be predictable
2. First born: Explain why
3. Second born: Give details
4. Third born: Show benefits

5. Fourth born: Issue challenges

Teachers may find themselves resisting one or more of these strategies because of their own birth orders. Onlies may rely on organizing rather than motivating. First borns may expect children to do what they're told rather than informing them. Second borns may require the students to obey rules without question. Third borns may rely on motivating the children without challenging them. Fourth borns may expect children to figure things out for themselves.

TIME BY BIRTH ORDER

YOU KNOW PEOPLE who always seem to be late, sometimes extremely late. You make arrangements to do a project together and the person shows up an hour late. It seems some people cannot be on time no matter what they do. Some keep their clocks set fast to keep from being late. Some make it on time for a couple of events then are late for the next one. Friends compensate by telling the procrastinator an earlier time just so he'll get there at the right time. What is going on with the procrastinator? Birth Order helps answer the question.

Because of their organization, Onlies tend to be on time. They usually maintain a schedule in their heads and follow it. They don't like intrusion themselves so they don't want to intrude on someone else by being late. In fact, they often like to be early.

First Borns, living in a world where love is scarce, don't want to risk the loss of love by being late. However, they may find themselves not getting the time right so they arrive at the wrong time or even the wrong place. In paying attention to the other person's feelings, they may not pay adequate attention to the facts of time and place. They may also rely on assumptions about time and place based on what the other person usually expects rather than pay attention to the new arrangements.

Second Borns, driven by the need for perfection, tend to be on time. To be on time, they schedule themselves extra time so that something unexpected happening does not keep them from being on time. However, some Second Borns can be late because of commitment phobia. With commitment phobia, they try to avoid being trapped. If being on time represents being trapped they will be late on purpose.

Third Borns want to be on time but are often late because they fill their time with too many things. Their schedule is so tight that when something unexpected occurs they are forced to be late. Some Third Borns compensate by setting their clocks ahead by fifteen minutes so they will have extra time. It doesn't work because they know the clocks are fast so they take that into account.

Fourth Borns tend to be on time or way off. If they are on time, it is because they paid attention to the details. They listened. When they are way off, it is because they were thinking their own thoughts when the arrangements were made, not paying attention to the details.

The way to be on time is to pay attention to the details when plans are made rather than being caught up in thought. Tell yourself, "Never get so interested in thinking that you forget facts."

BIRTH ORDER VIEW OF OTHERS

THERE IS A key word for each Birth Order:
>Only - Playmates
>First - Teachers
>Second - Coaches
>Third - Friends
>Fourth - Family

Each of these words can be used in a therapeutic statement:

Forget making yourself have playmates, just let yourself have playmates. (Only)
Forget making yourself have teachers, just let yourself have teachers. (First)
Forget making yourself have coaches, just let yourself have coaches. (Second)
Forget making yourself have friends, just let yourself have friends. (Third)
Forget making yourself have family, just let yourself have family. (Fourth)

These statements can be used in any way that brings them to the attention of the other person. They can be sent in an email, put on a Facebook page, spoken in person or over the phone, or they can be included in conversation. They are highly effective in improving relationships.

The Only could not have playmates as a child so the memories make Onlies feel they cannot have playmates as adults. They may either try too hard to play or be so serious they cannot relate comfortably. They need to let themselves have playmates.

The First Born is told "You're older, you should know better" often making the First Born into a know-it-all who is not open to learning from others. They need to let themselves have teachers.

The Second Born is made to feel inadequate by the First Born out-performing him or her. The Second Born cannot accept coaching on how to do better because that would accentuate the inadequacy. They need to let themselves have coaches.

The Third Born is made to feel vulnerable by the Second Born so that they see everyone as a threat to them rather than as potential friends. They need to let themselves have friends.

The Fourth Born is made to feel rejected within the family so that family closeness makes them uncomfortable often causing them to sabotage family relationships. Fourth Borns need to let themselves have family.

BIRTH ORDER IS ONLY ONE PART OF PERSONALITY

BIRTH ORDER IS only one part of personality. There are at least three other inputs: prenatal learning, values, and experience.

Every baby is born with personality that is developed in the womb. This personality with which a person is born appears to determine the general emotional mood of the person.

Birth Order is developed during the first year or two of life when the child discovers answers to three questions: "Who am I, who are all these other people, and what is going on here?" The answers to these questions comprise the content of Birth Order.

In answering the question of "Who am I?", the First Born sees self as the abandoned one, the Second Born sees self as the inadequate one, the Third Born as the threatened one, the Fourth Born as the rejected one, and the Only as the controlled one.

In answering the question, "Who are those other people?", the First Born sees others as unloving, the Second Born sees others as competitors, the Third Born sees others as threats, the Fourth Born sees others as adversaries, and the Only sees others as controllers.

In deciding "what is going on here", the First Born feels love going to others, the Second feels rejection of achievements, the Third sees conspiracy, the Fourth sees conflict, and the Only feels pressure.

Following the establishment of Birth Order, the next input to personality is in values that are absorbed from the family making the child decide what is important in life. These values interact with Birth Order to create behavior and whether the behavior is good or bad depends on the values the child has adopted. Values are created as parents and other caretakers react to certain behaviors and ignore others. The child learns to value behavior that results in attention, whether positive or negative.

The fourth stage of personality development is life-long learning. In this stage, the person learns from experience what works and what does not. This experience does not modify personality but rather challenges the person to get different results by doing the same things differently. For instance, a person who is punished for crimes becomes more skillful at committing crimes to avoid punishment rather than becoming different. A person who is rebuffed for being kind finds different ways to be kind rather than becoming unkind. Personality is resilient, not easily changed.

Birth Order provides the organizing structure for personality. As we understand Birth Order we are more able to determine the other facets of personality that enable us to make necessary changes.